ABOUT THE AUTHOR

Also by
NICHOLAS A. BASBANES

A World of Letters

Editions & Impressions

Every Book Its Reader

A Splendor of Letters

Among the Gently Mad

Patience and Fortitude

A Gentle Madness

ABOUT THE AUTHOR

Inside the Creative Process

By Nicholas A. Basbanes

Fine Books Press 2010
a division of Journalistic, Inc.

Fine Books Press
4905 Pine Cone Drive, #2
Durham, NC 27707

Copyright © 2010 by Nicholas A. Basbanes
All rights reserved.
Printed in the United States of America.

Book design and typesetting
by Kathryn Rosenbrock Haller.

ISBN 978-0-9799491-3-5
Library of Congress Control Number 2009942357

First printing

www.finebookspress.com
www.finebooksmagazine.com

For CVB, who has been along
for the whole ride.

Contents

Introduction ix
Stephen Ambrose 3
Margaret Atwood 10
Russell Baker 13
Jimmy Breslin 21
A. S. Byatt 27
Oleg Cassini 38
Michael Chabon 42
Tom Clancy 46
Walter Cronkite 50
Louise Erdrich 61
Robert Fagles 65
Penelope Fitzgerald 72
Richard Ford 77
Kaye Gibbons 81
Mikal Gilmore 84
Nadine Gordimer 88
Noah Gordon 92
Donald Hall 98
Joseph Heller (1984) 102
Joseph Heller (1997) 107

John Irving	112
Kazuo Ishiguro	116
Alfred Kazin	120
Louis L'Amour	138
Lynda La Plante	147
Doris Lessing	150
Joyce Maynard	154
Arthur Miller	159
Toni Morrison	167
Leonard Nimoy	171
Edna O'Brien	174
Kenzaburo Oe	183
Grace Paley	186
Mario Puzo	190
Margret Rey	194
Oliver Sacks	197
Neil Simon	201
Calvin Trillin	218
John Updike	221
Kurt Vonnegut	225
Alice Walker	231
Dorothy West	235
Acknowledgments	243
Sources	245

Introduction

For twenty-one years during the final quarter of the twentieth century, I wrote a weekly newspaper feature that allowed me to witness on a regular basis a pivotal period in the life of American letters. The very nature of the approach I chose—face-to-face interviews with major authors—put me in direct contact with an extraordinary range of writers representing the full gamut of literary expression. For a person who has always considered the craft of writing and the publishing of books to be the ultimate calling, it was a privilege that I never took for granted, and the skills I developed while engaged in this exhilarating pursuit contributed measurably to the author I have become in my own right.

It started simply enough in the form of a column I was expected to write as one of my regular duties while employed by the *Worcester Telegram* and *The Evening Gazette*, two competing newspapers under single ownership in Central Massachusetts that, in 1988, were merged into one daily publication, the *Telegram & Gazette*. After seven years of general news reporting for the *Gazette*, a good deal of it investigative work, I was named *Telegram* book editor in 1978, my principal responsibility to oversee a comprehensive section of reviews and commentary for the *Sunday Telegram*.

As a secondary assignment—on my old aircraft carrier we would have called it a collateral duty—I wrote a weekly piece for the Wednesday *Gazette* on a subject of my choosing, the one requirement being that it have something to do with books. One of my predecessors in this position had been a man named Ivan Sandrof, a well-known figure in the cozy world of New York publishing who, in 1974, had founded the National Book Critics Circle, and served as its first president. (Since 1981, in fact, the NBCC board has given out an Ivan Sandrof Lifetime Achievement Award to recognize notable contributions to American arts and letters, honoring such recipients as John Leonard, William Maxwell, Robert Giroux, Lawrence Ferlinghetti, and Pauline Kael.)

Ivan had also been something of a mentor to me during my years as a reporter, giving me dozens of books to review in a rich variety of genres and subjects, and later inviting me to become a charter member of the Critics Circle when he was just getting it off the ground. All of this gave me a leg up on the competition when I applied to succeed him for what I have said on numerous occasions became my dream job. How could it not be? I was already a bibliomaniac, and here, all of a sudden, new books of every description were being sent to me gratis by every major publisher in America, a harvest of riches arriving in each day's mail. Rarely has the expression "so many books, so little time" been more appropriate; I thought of it as an open-ended extension of my liberal arts education, and reveled in the plentitude of print.

At first my columns were a lot like the ones Ivan had written: succinct pieces of a certain length hammered out on deadline that listed a lot of the newly released titles of the day, spiced with generous dollops of bookish chit-chat. After a month or so of trying that, I decided this sort of desk-bound journalism was not for me, and I began to accept some of the offers I had been getting from New York publicists to meet with the front-list authors they were sending through Boston to promote their books. I have always enjoyed the rush and the immediacy of being out there in the field—once a reporter, always a reporter, I guess—and a good deal of the motivation, I am sure, was a desire on my part to once again be on the prowl for appealing stories. But mostly I was driven by an underlying desire to stake out my own turf and to shape my own identity as a columnist, which in the newspaper business means to establish your own voice.

It wasn't long before I was thinking of the pieces I was writing as a kind of literary feature, a hybrid type of journalistic concoction that combined the skills of an experienced interviewer with the considered analysis of an impartial critic. Typically, the two disciplines do not intermingle; a review is supposed to be a work of detached criticism, and a feature is a less structured and more stylistic sort of soft-news exercise, both of them traditional conventions, by the way, that I scrupulously imposed on the many freelancers I recruited to write for my Sunday pages. But on Wednesdays I was free to do as I wished, and I came to regard every column that I wrote as a performance unto itself, each mindfully conceived as a stand-alone narrative with a beginning, a middle, and an end, yet each consistent in tone and approach.

Because Boston has always been an A-list book town, every author of consequence came through on tour, and I had my pick of the field. Admittedly, I had a strong literary bent; I cared deeply about bringing to the attention of my readers well-written and important works of the imagination, and I am especially pleased to have noticed the work of authors such as Louise Erdrich, Scott Turow, Marilynne Robinson, Ethan Canin, and Howard Norman at the beginning of what in each instance has proven to be eventful careers. But I was ever mindful of the fact that I was writing for a general readership with multiple interests. So while there were numerous authors of high critical acclaim I profiled over the years—and a good number of them are represented in the pages that follow—there were many highly skilled genre writers I respected tremendously, too, people like P. D. James, Robert B. Parker, James Lee Burke, and Ruth Rendell, who had interesting things to say about what they do so well.

As a person drawn professionally to nonfiction, having an opportunity to talk shop with such superstars as Barbara Tuchman, David Herbert Donald, Theodore H. White, and David Halberstam—a full list is impossible in this brief space—was like being enrolled in a master class taught by the very best in the business. One of my earliest interviews with a Pulitzer Prize winner—the biographer Justin Kaplan, in 1981—yielded this nugget: "Biography is a form of story-telling. You aim to take the real life of someone no longer living and give it a literary life of its own. That is why I started with Mark Twain as he was leaving California and about to enter his years of greatness, and why I structured my life of Walt Whitman to imitate precisely the kind of metaphor that lies at the center of *Leaves of Grass*, a sense of eternal renewal."

I don't mind admitting to having had a weakness for meeting up periodically with celebrity authors such as Ansel Adams, Chuck Yeager, Buzz Aldrin, Joan Baez, and Elia Kazan. When I interviewed Julia Child over coffee and madeleines one morning in her Cambridge, Massachusetts, kitchen, I had no earthly idea that the table where we sat—and all the culinary knick knacks hanging on the walls around us—would one day be a prime exhibit in the Smithsonian Museum of American History in Washington, D.C. On those wonderful occasions when a renowned poet was available—Stanley Kunitz, Robert Creeley, Donald Hall, Allen Ginsberg, and the Polish Nobel laureate Czeslaw Milosz leap to mind—I got out a notebook, sharpened my pencils, and made sure there were fresh batteries in the tape recorder.

Not to be overlooked, either, is a little practice I followed in every instance; always, at the end of each interview, I asked the authors to write something in my copies of the books we had just discussed. Before long, a unique collection of inscribed first editions was taking shape; more important, a concept for what would become my first book began to emerge. I recalled in *Editions & Impressions*, the companion volume to this collection, how that came to pass, so I need not explore it further here, except to note that around the time that I had written my five hundredth author profile in 1988, I signed a contract to write *A Gentle Madness*, and that when I started doing the research for that book, my literary interviews began to take on an added dimension. All of a sudden I wanted to know more about "where all this stuff comes from"—what we call the creative process—fueling a line of inquiry that will be evident in many of the pieces that follow.

Another incentive came in 1991 when I left the *Telegram & Gazette* to concentrate more fully on my book in progress. I continued to write the newspaper column and began offering it to other outlets. My wife, Connie, and I established what we called the Literary Features Syndicate, and our game plan was pretty straightforward. Using the *Editor & Publisher* yearbook and *Literary Marketplace* as Baedekers, we targeted publications in university cities and state capitals, all of them well-read and informed communities where I was confident there would be interest in what I had to offer. I also had success getting into a number of independently owned newspapers where the feature editors were not required to clear all of their freelance decisions through corporate bean-counters.

At the height of my activity, I had stories running in more than thirty publications nationwide, some, like the *Philadelphia Inquirer*, *Milwaukee Journal*, *Des Moines Register*, *Minneapolis Star-Tribune*, *Cleveland Plain Dealer*, and *Wichita Eagle*, taking them on a selective basis, while others, like the *Toledo Blade*, the *Salt Lake Tribune*, New London (*Conn.*) *The Day*, the *Patriot-Ledger* in Quincy, Massachusetts, the *Knoxville News Sentinel*, *The Morning Call* in Allentown, Pennsylvania, and, of course, the *Telegram & Gazette*, never missing a week. "That's quite a nifty little string of papers you've got there," the legendary editor of *The Washington Post*, Ben Bradlee, said during lunch at Locke-Ober café in Boston, after he had asked me to name some of the places where my profile of him would be running. I once calculated the combined circulation of all these publications—and I included *Publishers Weekly*, the influential trade magazine for which I wrote about a dozen profiles that I later groomed into more compact columns for my newspaper clients—to be somewhere around three million, a number that gave some pretty decent exposure to a good number of the pieces I wrote.

Especially gratifying was the response I often got from readers, always a joy to receive, since nobody likes to write in a vacuum, and because feedback of any kind is one of the vital signs of the business. Sometimes it came in the most unlikely of places. John Irving, an author not prone to granting many interviews, told me when I arrived at his mountainside house in rural Vermont that he had agreed to see me because former colleagues of his from the Iowa Writers Workshop had been sending him clippings of my pieces from the *Cedar Rapids Gazette*. At a breakfast reception for members of the National Book Critics Circle held one morning in the Random House building, Ashbel Green, a greatly admired editor for Alfred A. Knopf, walked over to a group of people who were having coffee in a corner and asked if anyone among them might be Nick Basbanes. Me, I told him. "I read your columns all the time in *The [New London] Day*," he said, leaving me startled that he would even know my name.

All of this was heady stuff, but the biggest kick of all, without question, always came from the time I spent with the authors. The vast majority of them were pleasant enough, as should be evident in the verbatim transcripts that follow, though on a few rare occasions it was clear that we were together only because the publishing house had insisted upon it. Take special note in this regard of the dialogue with Alfred Kazin, where the atmosphere was tense, which nevertheless did not prevent me from walking away with a good story. My priority in the hour I was generally allotted with each writer, of course, was to nail down exactly that—the rudiments of a good newspaper story. But sixty minutes is a long time, and as I began to develop themes and strategies for my own books, I jumped at the opportunity to gather material that would have been available to me nowhere else. My favorite example of this sort of cross-fertilization appears in the concluding paragraph of the first chapter in *A Gentle Madness*, which I called "Touching the Hand." That phrase came up during a 1992 interview I had with the great Southern man-of-letters Reynolds Price, who used it to explain why he had acquired a rare copy of John Milton's *Paradise Lost* that had once been owned by the blind poet's daughter and amanuensis, Deborah Milton Clarke. "For me," Price said—and he was a dedicated Milton scholar who, like his subject, had suffered a health crisis at mid-career—"it was like the apostolic succession. I was touching the hand that touched the hand that touched the Hand."

It is no exaggeration to say that publishing has changed dramatically in the years since I stopped writing my literary features in 1999. Thousands of new titles are still issued every year, but the way publishers and authors go about letting the world know about them has shifted along with the times, especially since the book review itself has become a terminal species among so many newspapers, which themselves are under siege by advancing technology. Even the once inviolable author tour—certainly on the scale that it was once practiced—has been marginalized because of tightening budgets and declining media outlets.

Dipping into these conversations again, after all these years, was like going off on an archaeological dig and having one pleasant surprise after another emerge from the soil. To have a few of them come back to life now, within these pages, reminds me of a conversation I had with the incredibly prolific Isaac Asimov at a small dinner party given in New York in 1984 to commemorate the release of his three-hundredth book. I had asked this whirlwind of intellectual energy—a business card he gave me amusingly identified him as a "natural resource"—how it was possible for one person to be so inexhaustible in so many areas. "Nothing is wasted," he confided, tapping his forehead—and he would write or edit another two hundred or so books before he died eight years later—"and everything is in play." These, too, were words of wisdom that I appropriated as my own—and which I continue to apply to this day.

Nicholas A. Basbanes
North Grafton, Massachusetts
Thanksgiving Day 2009

ABOUT THE AUTHOR

Stephen Ambrose

*Interview conducted on December 8 and 9, 1995,
in Bay St. Louis, Mississippi, to discuss* Undaunted Courage.

As a writer who has devoted his professional life to the study of military history and the lives of notable American leaders, Stephen E. Ambrose has a keen eye for decisive moments, those make-or-break instants in which good luck can be as important as sound judgment.

The sixty-year-old Mississippi scholar's eighteen books have included multivolume biographies of Dwight D. Eisenhower and Richard M. Nixon, a penetrating study of the parallel lives led by General George Armstrong Custer and Chief Crazy Horse, and a riveting narrative of the Allied invasion of Normandy on June 6, 1944. *Undaunted Courage*, from Simon & Schuster, is an absorbing account of the Lewis and Clark expedition commissioned by Thomas Jefferson 193 years ago, and it takes full advantage of recent scholarship on the intrepid band of soldiers that Meriwether Lewis and William Clark led across the American West.

"I always try to look at whatever I'm writing about as both a biographer and a historian," Ambrose says during a cordial tour of the large office he maintains behind Merry Weather, his modern house in Bay St. Louis, Mississippi, an Old South community an hour's drive east of New Orleans on the Gulf of Mexico. On the walls and shelves are a variety of photographs, maps, posters, antique firearms, busts, statuettes, and knickknacks, all related in one way or another to the various books he has written over the past thirty-four years.

"I find that people who make key decisions, whether they're political or military, are not just fascinating characters in their own right, but so consequential. The impact of the individual on the situation—from squad level through high command in wartime on to the White House—is the same. The mistake that a person makes at a critical time, or the right choice that is made, is a very important part of how I try to meld history and biography. For my own part, I think that the two disciplines are one."

Significantly, Ambrose cites an encounter from his own youth as an example of how chance events can profoundly determine the future. In 1962, Louisiana State University Press published his first book, a biography of Army General Henry W. Halleck, President Lincoln's wartime chief of staff. "I doubt that they ran off a thousand copies, but one of them found its way to Dwight Eisenhower," Ambrose says between deep drags from one of the Marlboro Lights he smokes with undisguised satisfaction. "Talk about a life-changing incident; Ike phoned me one day and asked me to visit him at his farm in Gettysburg." After a lengthy chat, the Supreme Commander of Allied Forces in Europe during the Second World War and the former two-term President of the United States offered Ambrose, then twenty-six years old, an opportunity to assist in the editing of his papers and to write his authorized biography. "I asked Ike, 'Why me?' and he said, 'I read your book on Halleck.' He really could have knocked me over with that."

With a Ph.D. in history from the University of Wisconsin, Ambrose was at that time an assistant professor at the University of New Orleans. In 1964, he received a teaching appointment at Johns Hopkins University in Maryland, where Eisenhower's brother, Milton, was president, and where a team of scholars had been assembled to edit the general's papers.

The arrangement kept Ambrose within close driving distance of Gettysburg, where he was able to conduct numerous personal interviews with Eisenhower. "Ike had the most fabulous ability to concentrate," Ambrose recalls. "He would lock his eyes right on me and put his mind fully on every question I asked. There was never a look to the watch, never a straightening of clothes, never a call for coffee."

The first five volumes of *The Papers of Dwight David Eisenhower* were published in 1967 by Johns Hopkins University Press; fifteen volumes have appeared thus far in the series. Ambrose's first biography of Eisenhower, *The Supreme Commander: The War Years of General Dwight D. Eisenhower*, was published by Doubleday in 1970, the same year he returned to the University of New Orleans and became a full professor. The move from an academic press to a trade house was made without the assistance of an agent, Ambrose points out, for a simple reason: "It's pretty easy when you've got exclusive access to General Eisenhower."

Ambrose published two more books about Ike with Doubleday. When his editor there, John Ware, left to form his own literary agency, Ambrose went with him as a prize client. An auction for his next book was immediately announced, with the winning bid tendered by Alice E. Mayhew, vice president and editorial director of Simon & Schuster. "It was by far the biggest advance I'd ever gotten." In 1983, *Eisenhower: Soldier, General of the Army, President-Elect, 1890–1952*, the first of eleven books Ambrose has done with Mayhew, was published to widespread acclaim. So strong is his relationship with Mayhew that he dismissed his agent years ago and negotiates all of his publishing contracts himself.

"I admire her so much," he says, making no bones about the fact that he writes with the single-minded idea of trying to please Alice Mayhew. "She's my target audience. She's fast-track New York, extraordinarily bright, very opinionated, and terrifically good at what she does. Mostly, what I learn from her is what works and what doesn't. She can pick out the superfluous paragraph, or sentence, or word better than anybody, but she never tries to tell me what to say. She's an absolute genius."

Ambrose credits Mayhew with persuading him to write a series of books about Richard Nixon, a man he told her he "detested" when she broached the idea. "She said, 'There's no Nixon biography, and you're the perfect person to do it.' I said, 'Alice, I don't want to spend maybe five years with that son of a bitch,' and she said, 'Steve, where could you find a greater challenge?' She kind of caught me with that line." In due course, Ambrose furnished for her approval *Nixon: The Education of a Politician, 1913–1962* (1987), *Nixon: The Triumph of a Politician, 1962–1972* (1989), and *Nixon: The Ruin and Recovery of a Politician, 1973–1990* (1991).

Ambrose admits to never liking Nixon, whom he did not meet in person until after the three books were written. But he came to admire and respect him, "which was the biggest surprise of my whole writing career," recalls Ambrose, who has voiced his chagrin over the creative license taken in *Nixon*, Oliver Stone's film about the late president's life. "If Stone wants to say this is history, then damn it, he has an obligation to honor the integrity of the past."

In the midst of numerous successes came work on a novel that recreated the Lewis and Clark expedition through the imagined recollections of one of the enlisted men who participated. Ambrose declines to say why it was never published as a novel. "Alice told me to go back to writing what I do well."

The result of that advice is *Undaunted Courage: Meriwether Lewis, Thomas Jefferson, and the Opening of the American West*, a book Ambrose flatly declares to be a "labor of love."

Asked to explain the genesis of the project, Ambrose says that, "as a rule, I get my subjects by getting a curiosity, the only way to satisfy it is to write my own book." In 1975, Ambrose and his wife, Moira, decided they should spend the nation's bicentennial with their five children at Lemhi Pass in the Rocky Mountains, where Meriwether Lewis was the first non-Native American to cross the Continental Divide, in 1805. What most whetted Ambrose's interest was the gift of an early edition of the journals kept by Lewis and Clark on the two-and-a-half-year expedition.

"I am embarrassed to say that I had never read Lewis and Clark before that. I took one look and said, 'Wow, I've just got to go.' We began making plans immediately." After their first trip in 1976, the Ambroses have returned every year since.

"Every summer, we managed to get back to Montana, or Idaho, or the Dakotas, or Oregon, or Kansas to follow some part of the trail." The family has canoed 165 miles down the Missouri River, backpacked through the wilderness, horsebacked along the Lolo Trail, and turned in at night at various Lewis and Clark campsites. Three Ambrose children attended the University of Montana and now live in the state. Last year, when Ambrose took early retirement from the University of New Orleans, he bought a summer house in Helena.

Although the inspiration to write about Lewis and Clark can be traced back twenty years, Ambrose said other, more pressing projects always got in the way. Of particular urgency was his desire to finish *D-Day, June 6, 1944: The Climactic Battle of World War II* in time to coincide with the fiftieth anniversary of the Normandy invasion. That book drew heavily on 1,400 oral histories compiled by the Eisenhower Center for American Studies, which Ambrose has directed since its establishment at the University of New Orleans in 1983.

"When I finished the D-Day book, I decided it was time to concentrate on Lewis and Clark. I started by looking at what my strengths are. I know a lot about the U.S. Army. I know the Washington scene, which is virtually the same today as it was two hundred years ago. I know how to write a biography, and I am a serious student of what qualities go into making a great leader. I decided the best approach was to focus on one of the captains." What elevates Meriwether Lewis above most of his contemporaries, Ambrose emphasizes, is leadership, the very quality that has been the focus of his life's work. "To command with distinction is a rare talent, and studying it has been a passion for me."

In 1992, Ambrose received a fan letter from another eminent military commander, General Colin Powell, then Chairman of the Joint Chiefs of Staff. Powell had just read *Band of Brothers*, Ambrose's engaging book about the valiant exploits of an elite company of men in the 101st Airborne Division in Europe during the Second World War. The letter began a relationship that continues to this day. Last year, Ambrose championed Powell as a candidate for the presidency and spoke publicly on his behalf.

When Powell announced last fall that he would not seek elective office, Ambrose was disappointed. But he remains hopeful about a future candidacy. "Powell is a genuinely great man. He's a great leader, and in my opinion, the best man America has produced in this century. He has the qualities of leadership that are unique and blessed. I don't use the word *unique* the way television reporters do. I judge this by his character, by his personality, and by his experience. This is my deepest belief: Colin Powell is going to be President of the United States, and it's going to be a great day for us, and a great day for the world."

A native of Illinois, Ambrose did his undergraduate study at the University of Wisconsin and played football for three Badger teams during the 1950s. When he goes outside with *PW* to shoot some photographs at Merry Wether, Ambrose wears a crimson and white jacket with a big "W" sewn on the chest. "I was the last Big 10 player to play a full sixty-minute game," he says proudly.

"I was left guard on offense, a middle linebacker on defense, and if I had been ten pounds heavier, I'd have taken a shot at the pros. If I'd have done that, my life would have taken an entirely different course, and I doubt very much that I would have written any books.

Call that another example of good fortune. I firmly believe that history is chance, just like evolution. It's not survival of the fittest, it's survival of the luckiest."

Margaret Atwood

*Interviewed in New York City on February 15, 1995,
to discuss* Good Bones and Simple Murders.

When Margaret Atwood writes a novel, responsible readers everywhere pay attention. As one of Canada's two most prominent authors—she and Robertson Davies enjoy enormous international reputations—her work unfailingly occasions prominent notices in publications throughout the world.

Her best known book, *The Handmaid's Tale* (1985), depicted a bleak totalitarian society of the future in which women are denied all rights and became the basis of a motion picture; other notable works include *The Edible Woman* (1969), *Surfacing* (1972), *Lady Oracle* (1976), *Life Before Man* (1979), *Bodily Harm* (1981), *Cat's Eye* (1988), and *The Robber Bride* (1993).

While undeniably a champion of feminist causes, Atwood suggests in her work that it is women who must resolve women's problems, and she never lets ideology get in the way of good writing. Wit, irony, and tight control of form, combined with a fascination for classical and popular mythologies, have always characterized her style.

In addition to novels, Atwood is a prolific poet, critic, and writer of short stories, and has won every major literary award in Canada. In the United States, her books routinely command lead reviews in major journals, and appear often on bestseller lists.

One of the great pleasures in an Atwood book is that nothing she does is predictable. Indeed, her latest effort, *Good Bones and Simple Murders*, is a perfect case in point, since it is virtually impossible to categorize. Her publisher calls the compact volume of thirty-five pieces a "delightful collection of parables, monologues, poems, science-fiction adventures, postmodern fairy tales."

Though by no means Atwood at her strongest, it does have its place in the oeuvre. "They're complete pieces, and they're far too condensed linguistically to be considered journalism," the fifty-five-year-old Toronto resident stressed in a recent interview during a brief visit to New York.

"One of the problems is that they're not classifiable—you can't say that it's a novel or a short story or a poem—and because they're not classifiable, American publishers just don't know what to do with them." Europeans, on the other hand, readily accept the form, she said. "The French would probably call them prose poems; Kafka might call some of them parables."

"I would not describe these as diversions," she said. "These are pieces that I write from time to time, and they usually appear first in magazines, and I read them at readings where they're perfect, because they're so self-contained, and they're very popular with creative-writing teachers. They take them into their classrooms as an example to the students of something that they can do."

Some of the pieces present feminist themes with a light, amusing touch. In "Women's Novels," she pokes fun at the conceit that certain types of books, usually inferior, are written for women. "In men's novels, getting the woman or women goes along with getting the power. It's a perk, not a means. In women's novels, you get the power by getting the man."

Atwood's interest in mythology, folklore, and fairy tales is apparent in a number of the selections. "Unpopular Gals," for instance, gathers all the ugly stepsisters and wicked stepmothers for a kind of therapy session. "It's true," one complains, "there are never any evil stepfathers."

"Gertrude Talks Back" is narrated by none other than Prince Hamlet's mother, Queen Gertrude of Denmark. "I always thought it was a mistake, calling you Hamlet," she begins. "I mean what kind of a name is that for a young boy? It was your father's idea. Nothing would do but that you had to be called after him."

"The reader of these pieces does not have to be familiar with my work," Atwood said. "But the reader has to be familiar with *Hamlet*, say, or 'The Little Red Hen Tells All.' You figure everybody knows that fairy tale, but in fact, when it was translated into German, it was very funny, but they had never heard of 'The Little Red Hen.' It's not a known German story. So I found myself having to explain what the story was in the original, and now there's all these German academics analyzing 'The Little Red Hen.'"

These days, Atwood said she is "wrestling with a novel," and by wrestling she means "waking up at four in the morning and thinking." The fact that there is what amounts to an "Atwood industry" in literature departments throughout the world comes along with being taken seriously, but Atwood said she will leave the analysis of her work to others.

"I'm not an academic doing a thesis on myself, thank heavens, and for those who might want to do such a thesis, I'm not going to help them out. I'm not going to tell them." Why? "Because none of this really has anything to do with me, does it? You can't get too hooked on your career image."

Russell Baker

Interviewed on October 7, 1982, in Boston, for Growing Up, *an autobiographical memoir that went on to win a Pulitzer Prize.*

Russell Baker's column is a regular feature in these pages, so most of you may think you know quite a bit about this clever man already. His careful prose has an effortless flow to it, and like all good humorists, he rarely fails to snare a smile. Three years ago, he received a Pulitzer Prize for distinguished commentary, a validation of what millions of readers have known for years—he is the very best at what he does.

Week in, week out, he's there in the *New York Times* and hundreds of other publications around the world, sharp as ever. He's wise, he's insightful, he's graceful, he's sensitive, he's funny; these are all apt perceptions of the man. Baker has been writing his "observer" pieces now for twenty years. He does three a week, which works out to 140 a year, 2,800 all together. Each column is pegged at 800 words, give or take a few syllables, combining for a total word production over the years at somewhere in the millions.

The point here goes beyond arithmetic and the balancing of meaningless equations. What we're getting at is the formation of a persona in print. There is a continuity to a column; readers expect—indeed, they demand—consistency in tone and content, and Baker is no exception. His prose is gentle, unobtrusive, refined. Yet, despite his thousands of articles and millions of words, there is still much about the man we do not know, and that, Baker said over a long lunch in Boston last month, is by design, not by chance.

"I created a person for the column," he said. "In a sense, of course, it's me, but by and large I've kept my personal life to myself over the years." It's true, he acknowledged, that as he's grown older and become more self-confident, he has allowed more of himself to enter his writing. Readers, for instance, have been introduced on occasion to beguiling people named Uncle Hal and Uncle Charlie and Uncle Irvey. "I had been giving away bits and pieces about myself in the column. I found sometimes there were these people in me, trying to get out."

What slowly developed was the idea for a book, an autobiography, to be sure, but as it turned out, considerably more than that. *Growing Up*, published by Congdon and Weed, is certainly the story of Russell Baker's passage through childhood, but it is also the compelling, personal story of a tough period in history, the Great Depression, which is as much a character in this book as the people we meet. It is a remarkable memoir, above all, because it transcends the individual experience and recreates a time that is gone forever.

When you read the polished, refined, sophisticated sentences of Russell Baker, you think you're dealing with a proper, tweedy kind of man who's always led the same ordinary kind of life. "There has been that general impression among people who read me as being of the white-shoe set, a guy who went to Princeton and came down to Boston to write these stories," he said. "But I don't think about the image all too much, because the column has assumed its own identity. A column represents a person, but it isn't really that person. You speak with a certain voice, and after a while, it begins to capture you. When you try to break away from it, it disturbs the readership."

The idea to write about his coming of age in Morrisonville, a small village in rural Virginia, and to peel back, like an archaeologist unearthing layers of an ancient city, his memories of childhood, developed, paradoxically, from the securely happy lives he saw his three children leading. "There I was in middle age, looking at my children, and all I could think of was malice and envy," he said with a light chuckle. "I didn't have any luxuries, I never had any television. I really wrote this book because I wanted to tell my kids what America was like when I was a kid."

When you read books for a living, as I do, you're often asked how you go about deciding whether you like something or not. Obviously, there are many tests you have to apply, but one rule of thumb, ruthless as it may seem, which proves generally reliable, is whether the author is able to capture your attention in his very first paragraph. Here's how Russell Baker begins *Growing Up*:

> At the age of eighty, my mother had her last bad fall, and after that her mind wandered free through time. Some days she went to weddings and funerals that had taken place half a century earlier. On others, she presided over family dinners cooked on Sunday afternoons for children who were now gray with age. Through all this she lay in bed but moved across time, traveling among the dead decades with a speed and ease beyond the gift of physical science.

Though Lucy Elizabeth Baker was always a small, light-boned, delicately structured woman, she had the tenacity and will of a pit bull, with zeal and determination to match. Despite their poverty, despite the troubled times, she was always urging young Russell to "make something of yourself." A school teacher before her marriage to a handsome, hard-drinking stonemason, she was always using pithy maxims from the classroom to get her message across. To this day, Baker says, one-liners like "quitters never win" are "still tacked up in the back walls of my mind."

She was a "formidable" woman, he writes, determined "to speak her mind, determined to have her way, determined to bend those who opposed her." In his memory, she never sauntered. "She ran after squawking chickens, an axe in her hand, determined on a beheading that would put dinner in the pot. She ran when she made the beds, ran when she set the table…Life was combat, and victory was not to the lazy, the timid, the slugabed, the drugstore cowboy, the libertine, the mushmouth afraid to tell people exactly what was on his mind whether people liked it or not."

If Russell—or "Buddy," as he was called as a youngster—would prove to be the fulfillment of her aspirations, shameful failure came with her inability to "break" her husband Benny's profound appreciation for hard moonshine whiskey. In 1930, when Russell was just five, his father was taken to a hospital.

Buddy was off by himself, wandering down a dirt road near a creek, when two playmates caught up with him to report cruelly that his father was dead and that he should return home immediately. "He is not, he is not," the boy screamed, but deep inside, he knew they were right.

One of the many admirable strengths of *Growing Up* is the marvelously evocative way Baker is able to recapture the thoughts, emotions, and words of a boy who lived some fifty years ago.

"I've told people often about my father's death," Baker said. "That day is the first clear memory I have. Before that, everything is fragments, though I have many mental snapshots of my father. He was an absolute hell-raiser. I remember that clearly. I know I had been aware of death before that day, but it had never touched me. I understood then how terribly final it was. Starting from that point, the day he died, my life unfolds in one long narrative."

Baker recalls the tears that streaked his face that day for a number of reasons: "After that day, I never cried with any real conviction, nor expected much of anyone's God except indifference, nor loved deeply without fear that it would cost me dearly in pain. At the age of five, I had become a skeptic and began to sense that any happiness that came my way might be the prelude to some grim cosmic joke."

With her husband's death, Lucy Elizabeth had no desire to stay any longer in Morrisonville; in fact, there were any number of sensible reasons persuading her to leave, not the least of which was the fact she and her mother-in-law disliked each other intensely. Penniless, she decided to move to Newark, New Jersey. Russell and a sister, Doris, went with her; the youngest child, Audrey, was "given away" for adoption to a childless aunt and uncle.

Baker's feelings toward childhood—at least the way it had to be endured during the Depression—are ambivalent. "As far as I'm concerned, the idea that childhood is the best time of your life is a lot of baloney. You're bullied by your parents until you go to school; when you get to school, you spend your time in a freeform kind of jail. The bells ring, you're marched here, you're marched there. Childhood is entirely overrated as a happy time of life."

In Newark, Baker's mother came close to remarrying. Her intended was an affable Dane named Oluf, "a big, yellow-haired, outgoing man in his late forties, and a widower." A baker, he came to visit often, "arms filled with bags of pastries, which he jovially pressed on Doris and me." But the times got tougher, and Oluf left town in search of other work. One of the most powerful sections in the book is Baker's verbatim use of a series of letters Oluf wrote to Lucy.

At first, he is hopeful: "I always tell People not to worrie, so I won't either, now good Night with love to you and the Children from Oluf." But the months wear on, and increasing frustration is recorded in his correspondence, until the final blow is delivered:

> Dear Elizabeth, Thanks for your letter I received the other day, no you have not done anything to me, but the Deprescion has, the City took everything I hat for Taxes, so I am down and out, that is why I don't want you to write me any more... so Please forget all about me, I am lost and going...please try to feind a man good anof for you, and forget all about your ever seing Oluf."

Baker said he had discovered Oluf's letters years later. "My wife read them and thought it was a heartbreaking story of a man destroyed by the Depression. I gave them to my secretary to type and told her not to change a thing, none of the spellings, none of the punctuation. All that would do is get in the way of the story. I'm glad I didn't see any of her letters to him. I liked it better this way, because it was him and him alone.

"I had a great cast of characters to work with," Baker said. "I had nineteen natural uncles and two aunts." In developing the book, he conducted formal interviews with his key people and recorded what many of them had to say on tape. "I approached my life as a reporter would approach it," he said. "I got miles of tape with all these people talking about me. But after a while, I found I hadn't really interviewed the central figure in the story, which was me. I was keeping myself out of the copy. I didn't interview Russell Baker at the beginning, and that was a mistake."

A first draft of the book, completed last year, reflected this problem. "I finished it in July of 1981 and put it away. After a few months, I took it out, read it, and found it was putting me to sleep. It was there I decided the only way to do this was to examine myself, and that's where the book began to get very personal. What you see here is the second version."

If there is an "art to autobiography," he said, it is contained in one word: omission. "When you decide to write about your life, there are a million things you remember. What you have to do is organize everything in your head, find the meaningful patterns, and leave out what doesn't fit in."

Is confession good for the soul, he was asked.

"I am really not in favor of too much truth," he said. "A Frenchman once said the problem with Americans is they insist too much on telling the truth. He was talking specifically about love and sex, of course, but he felt this was our national problem, the idea that we have to confess so much about ourselves."

One potentially difficult problem, he found, was where to draw the line on what personal information he could include about his wife. "She had a really interesting childhood, too, and I was always mindful that I might be treading on her copyright. When I interviewed her, I could tell the areas she didn't want to talk about; I could tell when she was lying, as a matter of fact. But I wanted to get it right."

He decided Mimi would see none of the material about herself until it was finished, but that she would have the option of deleting anything about herself that she didn't like. "As it turned out," he said, "she told me I didn't put in enough about her. You can't win."

Lucy Elizabeth never stopped exhorting her son toward achievement. A scholarship at Johns Hopkins University was followed by several years of gainful employment with the *Baltimore Sun*. In 1954, he joined the Washington bureau of the *New York Times* and spent the next eight years reporting on public affairs. In 1962, he wanted to "break out of the *Times* straitjacket and deal with this material in a voice that ordinary people could understand."

Thus came the inspiration for his column. "When I started it, all I had in mind was writing about important events in a voice that would have a wide audience. Only later, when I discovered myself being called a humorist, did I realize that I was using satirical techniques. I never considered myself as being funny or being about to make people laugh; I was only interested in making them read. I did know that if I could make them smile, I could keep them reading. And that's pretty much where I am today. I accept the judgment that I am a humorist."

In 1974, Baker moved his family from Washington to New York. "I decided that twenty years there was long enough." And with time, he noted, his column evolved subtly. "As I've become older, it's become older. I am much more self-confident now, and it has become more personal in a sense. I find, too, I'm not afraid to discuss any issues now, as I was when I was a kid. I really didn't discuss anything controversial like abortion fifteen years ago. Now I do."

Though *Growing Up* gets most of its emotional thrust out of sad times, it does end with a warm story. Baker's marriage to Mimi, a vivacious woman who minced no words over her mixed feelings about Lucy Elizabeth.

"Let's get married," Baker tells her after a tempestuous courtship.

"Would I have to live with your mother?" she asks.

"That's a hell of a question."

"I just want to know whether I'm going to have a husband or a mother's boy."

With his mother's progression into senility—"hardening of the arteries" was the diagnosis—Baker often considers the meaning of her oft-repeated urgings to "make something" of himself. "She took great pleasure in my success, but never in my presence. She'd bore everyone to death over how proud she was, but never when I was around. In her old age, she took very little pleasure in her accomplishments. We showed very little physical emotion when I was a kid, and I grew up repressed and inhibited. I always found it difficult to express my love outwardly. I found it hard to tell my mother I loved her." If there is one enduring lesson he has learned from her, it is, he concluded, that "all your greatest ambitions are meaningless at the end."

Jimmy Breslin

Interviewed in Boston on September 16, 1996, to discuss
I Want to Thank My Brain for Remembering Me, *a memoir;*
Breslin won a Pulitzer Prize for commentary, in 1986.

Do you feel after your aneurysm that you're playing with house money, as Bill Cosby would say?

I guess so. It's a good line, but I never look at it that way. They say it's a beautiful day today. I never cared whether it was raining or snowing. It's a day; it gives you a shot at life, and it gives you another chance.

You look great.

I'm all right. I'm not drinking, I don't smoke. I live a lousy life as a result. The only thing that I liked to do was work and after work, right away, run into the bar, because after all, you just did a day's work, and you deserve a drink. So I used to drink a lot, and it was terrific. You tell lies at the bar and listen to stories. It was terrific.

One thing that went on in those newspaper saloons, which does not go on in New York anymore—I can only speak for New York—there's no bar anymore that everybody goes into. And in those bars, there was always somebody with a memory. Not the kind of cold, pitiless memory a computer drags up for you when you go to the files. I mean, they tell you a lot of addresses, but not much else. You have a guy at the bar who had covered something, had been around something; he could tell you what the weather was like and who was there and who talked and who said what away from the reporters, who got mad, who got drunk, who did this, and I remember that same day, this happened and that happened. You'd go into the bar and add to your lore, add to your knowledge, add to your experiences, and as you wrote, you could get the clips on the occurrence, and then you had the memory of the guy telling you about it to go with the clips, or the whaddya call it, the Lexis-Nexis [database].

I use everything in sight, but I still would love to have somebody who can tell me something about it orally. So, I think that's missing in the newspapers. They don't go to bars, they go home, all the people in the news business. They go home, or they go to health clubs. They have a glass of wine at home with dinner. I'm not knocking them, it makes a very healthy life; it makes a much better family life, but I think they're not as good reporters. And I think the readers get murdered because they are boring, and that's the number one sin in any religion—to be a bore. That's a felony.

What do you have to say about "pack journalism"?

It's crazy. I always ran away from the pack. When Kennedy—from this town—was killed in 1963, I went up the walk of the White House, and here was Haile Selaisse, from Ethiopia, in a pompous uniform with feathers and decorations, and next to him was Charles de Gaulle towering over him, wearing the uniform of a French non-commissioned officer. It was a great scene, but it was not good for me. I went into the White House, and I remember telling myself, "I've got to get away, there's three thousand reporters. I cannot make it here. What am I going to do?" And I said, "Well let's get to the central story. It's a funeral. The main thing in a funeral is burying somebody. So I'll go and get the guy who dug the grave." And I went inside for a moment, and Art Buchwald was there; he's from the *Herald Tribune*, the paper I was on. So I tell him, "I'm gonna go get the grave digger," and he said, "That is a good idea, that's a very good idea." I said thank you, and I left, fortified by his encouragement and his judgment. He's smart as hell.

I went to the cemetery, I found the gravedigger, his name is Paully. He got $3.10 an hour to dig the grave. He said it's an honor. He did it on a Sunday, his day off. Then the funeral came on, and here's Eisenhower, Truman, heads of state from all over the world, and Paully's dressed like a working man. They wouldn't let him in. Soldiers tell him to go away. You know, he wasn't dressed well enough. So he went and dug more graves—some serviceman from Somerville, now being buried as a soldier. He got $3.10, and he came back to the grave site when everybody was gone. He looked at it. He knew they needed some new turf here, and he would fix that, and he said it was an honor. And that for me was running away from the crowd. Always run away. Run for your life away from a crowd, because I think the public is lied to. When you get five cameras on somebody, and they're talking, you know the guy is only talking for himself. He's not trying to tell anybody anything. He's not going to give you anything new, which is the word for news. So pull your cameras out of there, the man is only going to lie. Don't talk to him.

You've said that your tip for young reporters is that the camera always screws up good stories.

Yes, because the camera doesn't do any work. What it does is stand there, and it's an accomplice for a liar, and the liar usually is the politician.

Do you think you would have written a memoir without your medical experience?

I wouldn't have. Memoirs, that's not me. What happened is that I got this aneurysm discovered by sheer luck. Total accident. They were looking for something else and they found this, and the thing they were looking for was a nothing.

I'm not going to go through all this and not use it. So I started to write it, and I started to write everything that happened to me on the day I went to get the top of my head taken off in an operation in Phoenix, Arizona.

This book is about surviving an aneurysm.

Most people don't even know what the hell it is. I didn't know what it is except from reading newspaper obituary stories. My anterior communicating artery right across the front of the brain had a blister on it. It's a blister; it looks like a blowout on a tire. This one was weak. You could see blood coursing through it, swirling. That's it. They operated, and I was very worried about coming out. I went through days, after I found out I had this thing, when I just assumed it would come apart. It never happened, and as the day of the surgery came on me, I grew calmer and calmer. I had a faith in God and a deep belief all my life.

I spent all of my life in newspapers and writing on poor neighborhoods, people of color. All people in trouble live on the fifth floor of a walk-up. There's nobody in trouble on the first and second floor. Five and six up. All trouble is upstairs. Start walking now. I can never get anything easy. So I thought that had a lot to do with it. I just thought that all those days and all those nights had done something for my soul, and I'm now getting some help out of it. I believed it was the state of grace. That's a Catholic belief.

Are you a regular churchgoer?

I am, yeah, 80 percent of the time. It sure reinforced my thinking.

The greater fear for you was that you would lose your ability with words, not life or death.

The aneurysm was right in front of the brain, that's where your language comes from. That was a big worry. Should have had me terrified, but it didn't until it got to one point after the operation.

There was a guy, you held up anything, and he'd say, "That's a taxicab." A jacket, and he said, "That's a taxicab." My kids saw that part. When I woke up from this thing, when I woke up from the operation, the minute I could, I tried to write. I wanted to write. I started to write something out. I really tried, and then it tired me. Pure Croatian, the thing I'd written. It was unintelligible. Then I thought there was something the matter with me. I became overwhelmingly depressed. And then the thought came to me, if I can see something is wrong, then I must have a way to fix it, to do it right. So I said, come on, there's only a living depending on this. I worked and finally I got one subject, verb, object, period to slip out of a Cross pen and a paper. I worked and another one appeared, and finally I got a paragraph down.

I like the line in there where you said you get your news on the 2 train. You don't drive a car?

When I started, most of the kids didn't have cars because the bus stopped right in front of my house, and the subway was close enough to walk to, and we had two els, a subway, and a bus. And I was working nights in a newspaper. I'd drink till 4 A.M. and then order thirty-two beers. The hangovers! When they started going into the second day, late into the second day, I said that's it for me. I can't do anything with a hangover, I'm a zombie. And if it's going to go two days, then it can go three, and that's it, goodbye.

You've given up you column, is that right?

I'm under contract for five years to the *Los Angeles Times* syndicate, and I'm supposed to write periodically, and that's what I do.

Do you miss it?

No, because I'm doing another book. It's a novel, I don't know what it's even about yet. We'll see. Novels are the most fun, the hardest work, and the riskiest.

Why are they more work?

Because there's not one scene that you don't have to make up yourself, and at the same time, it's got to be based on more fact and truth than a news story. You've got to have an awful lot of research for a novel. Then they can all criticize and call you names. It's great.

A. S. Byatt

Interviewed in Boston on May 31, 1996, to discuss Babel Tower. *Byatt's 1990 novel,* Possession, *won the Booker Prize.*

You are doing a quartet of novels. Could you tell me a little bit about the motivation for that?

I think first I had the idea of writing a sort of long novel, partly because I was reading Proust when I was at college, or just after. Then I had this idea that I had lived through a little bit of history, what with the war and the 1950s. So I thought I would write a longish novel with several main characters, and then it became a quartet. The idea was originally to have the first one, which was *The Virgin in the Garden*, as a kind of nostalgic looking back to the days of Shakespearean English, and possibly also the big nineteenth-century novel. Then I was going to do two more experimental ones. First was *Still Life*, which was going to be what I thought of as my biological novel, describing birth and death very, very barely and precisely. Then this one was always meant to be the linguistic novel, which is why it is called *Babel Tower*. It was meant to be the one about how language flew apart into fragments. It was called *Evidence* for a long time when I was thinking about it, then it came to its real name, *Babel Tower*. Then after that all those metaphors of towers began to proliferate all over it.

Did the title come while it was a work in progress?

Yes, it came probably at the end of the Eighties or the beginning of the Nineties.

How long was *Babel Tower* in progress?

I've been thinking about it, bits of it, since 1963. And when I've done the fourth one, that will be the end. I'm pretty sure, because I've got another two books after that that I want to write. I hoped to write it in the 1970s, but all sorts of things intervened and got in the way. I didn't mean to be writing it as late as this, the mid-1990s. I think it's probably on balance gained from me having been thinking about it for twenty-nine years rather than writing it.

So do you write it, then, with the perspective of a woman in the 1990s?

Oh, I think so. There is a different sort of ironic distance from the characters in the world than there would have been if I had written it earlier.

How do you think it would have been different had you done it in the Seventies?

There were a lot of things in the late Sixties and early Seventies that I found rather tedious and repulsive, like the theater of cruelty. It wasn't my favorite sort of theater. And all this idea that you should believe the Marquis de Sade and all the need to live in communes. I found most of these not my sort of thing and not what I had been hoping for. Whereas now all that seems to me much more coherent as a set of movements and as a kind of spectrum of moral interest and moral anxiety. From the immense sense of everybody loving everybody in whatever way they felt they could—"All you need is love," as the Beatles said—at one end, and the sort of people like Peter Brook in the theater, the impresario putting on the Marquis de Sade directing a madman in the performance in the *Death of Marat* [*The Persecution and Assassination of Jean-Paul Marat as Performed* by the Inmates of the Asylum of Charenton Under the Direction of the Marquis de Sade]. That was written by Peter Weiss. It was done to sort of upset and shock the audience and to send great frissons of pleasure and cruelty through your blood.

I couldn't find a copy of it anywhere when I was writing this book in the 1990s, and I finally got hold of one. It's actually a very static and boring play, I think. It's a brilliant idea. The Marquis de Sade did put on plays in his lunatic asylum in Charenton. It could have made a wonderful play. When you actually read the play, as opposed to seeing Peter Brook's absolutely starved production of it, it reads a bit stiff and wooden, and it goes rambling off. There were many art forms in the Sixties that were very rambling. It was very rambling and sort of repetitive. Anyway, I find it much more interesting now than I did then because I see much more now how it fits into the way everything works.

Is the Sixties a fascinating decade for you?

Not more than any other. It has developed this kind of cult status, and I have talked to generations of students for whom the Sixties has a sort of wonderful image of freedom and bliss and daring. It didn't feel quite like that when you were living through it. It didn't feel different from any other time. I think it's partly just a myth. Somebody said there are about a thousand people who were the Sixties, and all of them have written their reminiscences, saying that everybody was doing what they were doing—actually a thousand sounds just about right.

That's not a bad idea for a monograph or even a book.

Exactly. And you get a really top-notch photographer to take pictures of them all.

Have you thought of this?

It's not my sort of thing, I just want to get on with my novels. But it's a nice idea. I'm just trying to think who said it.

Did Timothy Leary die?

He died today.

I've been thinking about him, partly because I've been talking to journalists and bookshop people. I saw that he was conducting his death in public.

Do you see your books as a corpus, as a body of work?

What? All my work?

Yes.

Well, I haven't said this before, but I had this interesting idea. I wrote *Possession*, which is set in the time of Darwin's writing of *On the Origin of Species*, in 1859. And then I wrote *Angels and Insects*. The insects bit hit in the 1860s, and the angels bit moves on into the 1870s and 1880s. I have a novel I want to write next when I finish the quartet that is about that kind of group of people in the 1890s and 1900s, I think from the point of view of a children's writer, like E. Nesbit. She lived in a world which contained all the geneticists who believed in eugenics and all the proto-socialists. She knew H. G. Wells very well. He tried to seduce her daughter. She knew George Bernard Shaw. It won't be like that, but that world. I've got a great historical run, and the one I want to do after that, which doesn't yet have a title, is about two women psychoanalysts. I wanted to do an American and a middle European. But I think I can't write an American, so I think I'll write an Englishwoman psychoanalyst, and in the time of Freud and Jung.

You have a pretty good American in *Possession*, though?

Well, I was rather fond of both my Americans in *Possession*, but I do know that they were brought out by being caricatures. I taught American literature for a long time, and I made Professor Crocker out of all the preoccupations of nineteenth-century American literature—you know, the kind of Gothic interest, the Edgar Allan Poe interest in mortality. He came out of all those communes sprinkled around the times of Henry James.

Do you write on a computer?

No, I write with a pen, which produces the kind of writing I like. I do my journalism on a computer. But I do it mostly by not looking at it and just thinking it in my head and typing it off the keys. I don't look at it much when I'm actually doing it.

Do you notice a difference in the writing?

Yes. Everybody says that computers make them write longer. They make me write much shorter. If it's a thousand-word review, whenever I do a word check, I quite often find I have said everything I want to say in 750 words; whereas if I'm doing it by hand, it will run over. It's nice to be able to push two keys and get an exact count.

Reviewing is like an art form. It's like the sonnet in one sense, it's got to be done precisely. And most reviews are about fourteen lines. There are a lot of young men reviewing in England at the moment who don't seem to realize that you can't quote extensively in a review of a thousand words, because it leaves you no time to say anything. They don't do it out of laziness, they do it because they have been taught close reading at university, and they feel they have to demonstrate their point. What they do is they pick out a paragraph which is part of the much larger structure, which of course they haven't left themselves space to describe (if they understood it), and then they say, "Look at that silly word in the second line of that paragraph, how could she use that word?" They make themselves look very clever, but actually what they're doing doesn't mean very much. It's always very lopsided because of that silly quote. Whereas where I grew up, in a thousand words you could quote one and a half lines, maximum, of what you're reviewing.

Today a thousand words is quite an indulgence.

A thousand words is about as big as you can get in a newspaper. I can do six hundred words, too. I can even do two hundred words. There the challenge is to say anything at all.

I really am interested in getting back to whom you are writing for. Do you have a reader in mind? I know you certainly have a very strong academic background, and I know you bristle at suggestions, rightfully so, that you are an academic who writes novels for a general readership. Perhaps you could address all of those concerns?

I've never thought of myself as an academic. When I was very young, I made a choice about whether to be an academic or whether to be a writer, and I did decide to be a writer. I taught university for eleven years, but that was mostly to earn money to put the children through school.

I used not to have a reader in mind very much. I mean, I used to say as a joke, if I was asked, "I write for Henry James." He has had a surprisingly large and durable readership of people who are not academics. Anyway, I used to think I was writing for him. You know, I used to think he would understand what I was trying to do. And now I do know that I have a lot of readers of very many different kinds. This makes you actually feel quite comfortable with yourself, because if you can write something as historical and as intellectual as *Possession* and become a bestseller, you can presumably do anything.

Did the success of *Possession* shock you?

I thought it would sell quite well. I would have guessed it would have sold 25,000 or so in the hardcover. In fact, it got itself up to 120,000, which is a big difference. But 25,000 is quite a lot. I knew it was a sort of good story that people would enjoy, and I got terribly upset when all the publishers tried to take all the things out. Writing *Babel Tower* was quite good, because I've done so many readings in so many countries, and people kept saying, "What's happened to Frederica? Why haven't you finished it?" I knew it had readers who were waiting for it.

I am really interested in how extensively writers are influenced by their reading, and I wonder whether you are quite a voracious

reader, perhaps even a bibliophile. Do you collect books, by the way?

I own a large number of books, but I only collect them for the contents. It would never occur to me to go out and look for a first edition. I should guess I have about 12,000 volumes. The house is full of books.

Does your reading influence what you write?

Oh yes. I feel that the great writers of the past are my ancestors, as it were. You can always learn something. And also, I think my books are as real to me as people. You get the sort of sense of a shape of a book. Occasionally, you'll go into a house, and there isn't a book. My mother-in-law had about eight books. They were books of poetry, and she read them and reread them with a great passion. How could she stop there and have just eight?

She had one little bookcase, with an arch over the top, and it had this row of books, and there were two or three 1930s novels, and in the back, half a dozen good books of poetry, and a gardening book, and that was it. I just can't imagine that. I feel that isn't quite a life.

Do you have books that you haven't read?

Not before. Now I do. I've got quite a lot of books that I haven't read, and these are of two kinds, three kinds really. They're the ones I've bought because I know I need them for my research, and I haven't yet got round to reading them. There are the ones I've bought because they look quite interesting, and I haven't got around to reading those as well. And then there are the ones that people send me, and in my position you get sent hundreds of books. Some of them come from the author saying, "Please write something for the back of my book." Some of those come from the publisher. One came from my own publisher not long ago.

The only way I can deal with all of this is to write back to absolutely every single one, even my best friend, and say, "No, I will not write anything on the back of anybody's book, ever." And I say that if I write a review, then obviously you can quote my review, but that's public. I don't like the private back scratching, and also the only way I can cope with the people is to make it quite clear to them that I won't even consider it.

Briefly, to get back to *Possession*, was that a liberating book for you in that it's been called the breakthrough book?
Yes, it was a breakthrough book, and it was a liberating book, partly because it actually was quite easy to write—although it looks very complicated—and partly because everybody liked it so much. Almost nobody disliked it, as far as I can see, which ought to make one a bit suspicious of it.

Are you fearful of so much public approbation?
Well, what I feel is that after that much public approbation, this sort of cut-and-thrust young journalist will decide that you need taking down a peg or two, that you need to be cut down to size. They think somehow that because you have been well received you must now be mocked, and this is very tedious. I've seen it happen to other people so much that I know it's not personal.

I'm not very good at being famous. On the whole, I would much rather be at home writing a book than being on a book tour. But it is nice having the money, apart from anything else.

What do you feel about books in the future? Do you have a sense?
I have two or three contradictory senses. I tell you, if you haven't happened to already have heard or seen it, George Steiner has been giving a brilliant series of lectures on books of the future. He gave a brilliant one I heard in Cambridge last summer, and he has a son who teaches—I think this is right—he has a son who teaches disadvantaged children in North Carolina, and he goes there with holograms and CD-ROMs. He can offer them the whole of the Library of Congress and the whole of the British Library on these CD-ROMs, although these kids do not have the money to buy a

book, and he said this is good. And he has a daughter who is an anthropologist or some sort of something, or Sinologist, I forget, but she is somewhere in Harvard or Yale, and she enviously communicates her papers by sticking them into the Internet and immediately getting comments back on e-mail. She's connected into the major people. Now this obviously is going to make a physical book less necessary, but I still think there will be physical books, because I think people will continue to want to carry them about in their pockets and read them in airplanes.

I think for literature, the book lives and that for research and the kinds of things you're describing right now, the computer kicks in.

Any of those things can be made into a book if you want it to. If you talk to scientists, they say there is no reason to publish in book form. Most scientific papers, it is enough that there should be an Internet register or a CD-ROM register with all the titles. I think they think that any scientist can then, as it were, clock into this and draw out any paper they want to read, and it need never be printed down in a book.

Tell me briefly, if you would, about this obscenity case you use in *Babel Tower*, and why that was necessary, particularly in the concept of this book?

It's partly because there were a lot of obscenity cases. It's a book that's essentially about the relationship of language to things and language to life and the way it gets torn apart. In the Sixties, I knew a lot of people who gave evidence both in the *Lady Chatterley* trial and in the trial of *Last Exit to Brooklyn*, and they were describing to me this sense they had that the whole of the language they wanted to use was being distorted by the legal process. They couldn't say what they would have liked to say. They were having to say something else. The whole process was driving them into talking in a different way. I got quite interested in that, and then, I wanted to contrast that sort of public distortion with the private distortion of a divorce, which in those days had to be adversarial. I was interested in courtroom narratives. I mean just as *Possession* is interested in detective stories and romantic love stories, this is interested in the nature of the courtroom narrative and how it changes the people.

There was a lot of argument over whether we should or shouldn't censor the Marquis de Sade, and the *Last Exit* case was lost because the jury brought a verdict against *Last Exit*. This was overturned on appeal, because I think all the lawyers felt on the whole that the book ought to be published, even the ones who were prosecuting. So the judge found various reasons, and *Last Exit* went through. But it's exactly that point. In 1967, the Moors murderers were tried [for killing five children near Manchester, England], and when they looked at [the suspect Ian] Brady's library, he had an extensive library of the Marquis de Sade and the Lindbergh trials and various other books about torture. That really frightened people. It produced a kind of feeling that perhaps these things were dangerous, when we just thought we were becoming more liberal and more free to publish everything.

There's a very interesting parallel today with the Unabomber. They're trying to look at what he read, and they're trying to find the books that he might have taken out of the University of Montana.

Oh, that fascinates me. Actually, the libraries of murderers are fascinating. The library of anyone, of course, is fascinating. Brady's library is completely recorded. There is an ancient Penguin transcript of the trial, written at the time of the trial, and they list the books that he was found to have.

Were you surprised by the American reaction to *Possession*?

No, I don't think I was. I always felt that my earlier books, if they had gone into paperback, the Americans would have liked them. And in fact when they did go into paperback, the Americans did like them. One of the good results of *Possession* was that *Still Life* then went into paperback and sat on the *New York Times* paperback bestseller list for quite a long time, which was unexpected. Nobody had bothered to put it into print. I think the thing about *Possession* appealing to the Americans that most pleased me was that they do seem to like all the others. All the others are now in print, and they are staying in print.

Do you hear from the readers?

Oh, I hear from the readers a great deal, and I very much enjoy it. It has made a great difference having all these American readers. I love talking to them in the bookshops, because they do take the books slightly differently than the English. The reviewers in many ways bear no relation to readers. It takes a few years of being reviewed for you to understand it. Reviewers have their own agenda. They have their own knowledge, and they come, I think, quite often with preconceptions about what it's going to be and what they're going to say, which the book doesn't always change, even if it should have done. Readers come all innocent and open. If they don't like your book, they just stop reading it. If they do like it, then they respond with generosity. It's much the best thing, really.

Oleg Cassini

Interviewed in New York City on October 5, 1995, for A Thousand Days of Magic: Dressing Jacqueline Kennedy for the White House.

Barely a month before John F. Kennedy took the oath of office as the thirty-fifth President of the United States, the New York designer Oleg Cassini was offered the most coveted fashion assignment of the century.

"In effect, I was handed a script," Cassini said during an interview in the exquisitely appointed townhouse he maintains near Gramercy Park, in New York City. When not in Manhattan, the legendary designer is usually at his summer house in Oyster Bay, on Long Island, New York. "I saw this as a play on Broadway, only here my job was to dress Jacqueline Kennedy for the leading role."

The role in question, of course, was that of First Lady, and the political equivalent of opening night came thirty-five years ago next month, during President Kennedy's inauguration. "It was an extraordinary opportunity; Jackie was going to be seen by the entire world," Cassini said. "I realized this was my chance to establish the *look* at the very beginning."

What Cassini calls the *look*—a luminous, almost ineffable, statement of grace, elegance, and savoir-faire—was unveiled on January 20, 1961, during the swearing-in ceremonies on the steps of the U.S. Capitol. It was a smashing success, so much so that Jackie Kennedy's distinctive style endures to this day, with continued attempts by a multitude of pretenders to replicate it.

"I tried in my mind to see the inauguration as a scene in a movie," Cassini recalled between appreciative puffs from a hand-rolled Havana cigar. "I said to myself, 'Well, all these other ladies are going to wear fur coats, and they will look like big grizzly bears, every one of them. I am going to have Jackie look like a young, beautiful, simple thing, so fresh, so pretty, so unpretentious.'"

The ensemble Cassini chose—a fawn-colored wool coat with sable trim at the collar and a matching pillbox hat that became something of a trademark—was completed with a sable muff that the First Lady added as her own finishing touch.

Over the next thirty-four months, Cassini would create some three hundred outfits for Mrs. Kennedy, about one every three-and-a-half days, each carefully conceived and crafted as part of an overall concept.

Cassini recalls this uncommon professional and personal experience in *A Thousand Days of Magic: Dressing Jacqueline Kennedy for the White House*, a beautiful book that includes 260 illustrations and excerpts from dozens of pertinent letters.

Cassini said he decided to write the book after Jacqueline Kennedy Onassis's death two years ago. "A lot of people in the fashion industry resented my appointment and did not want to acknowledge my contributions," he said, pointing out that until now he has been unable to document the extent of his influence on the official wardrobe.

"When Jackie was alive, she was always there to defend me. She was very loyal. But now, I felt I should offer my own perspective on these thousand days of magic. This book had to be written, because it's part of history. This was a lady who single-handedly created Camelot."

Cassini tells how he was summoned from a Nassau holiday to meet with the thirty-one-year-old First Lady-to-be a few weeks after the 1960 election and offered an opportunity to work with other famous designers. Cassini said that he balked at the idea and urged her to pick a single fashion adviser, whoever it might be.

"You need to stick with one person, someone who can create a look just for you," he recalls telling her. "I want you to be the most elegant woman in the world. I think that you should start from scratch with a look, a look that will set trends and not follow them." He said he would approach the task as if she were a movie star, an idea that proved irresistible.

Before making his name on Seventh Avenue in New York, Cassini worked in Hollywood as a costume designer. Married for a brief time to the actress Gene Tierney, and later engaged to Grace Kelly, he had dressed some of the most exquisite women in the world before getting the call to submit some sketches to Mrs. Kennedy.

Cassini's own noble lineage undoubtedly strengthened his appeal. The son of a pre-revolutionary Russian count and grandson of a Russian ambassador to the United States, he was born in Paris in 1913. He did his earliest fashion designs in Italy and moved to the United States in 1936. A skilled equestrian, he was an officer in the U.S. Cavalry during the Second World War.

Of critical importance to Cassini's selection as Mrs. Kennedy's designer, however, was his intention to create a total concept. Different outfits were necessary for different events, be they an audience with the Pope, lunch with the Queen of England, tea with Indira Gandhi, or a state dinner with Charles de Gaulle.

"I didn't want to create dresses for the sake of creating dresses, and the first two or three outfits that appeared were saluted by everybody," he said. "Even the French recognized that a new look had been born. I was very lucky, because if I had not done the job in the first two weeks, believe me, I was a goner. The woman demanded nothing but the best."

Although Mrs. Kennedy is legendary as a perfectionist, she gave people the freedom they needed to do their jobs. "It was the same with me as with the French chef she brought in," Cassini said. "She said to the cook, prepare me a menu, and just do it. Once I presented the sketches, and she liked them—and 99 percent of the time she liked them—she said do it. Just do it. That was the essence of our relationship. And it worked beautifully."

Michael Chabon

*Interviewed in Boston on February 6, 1996,
for* Wonder Boys; *Chabon won a Pulitzer Prize for fiction,
in 2001, for* The Amazing Adventures of Kavalier & Clay.

Michael Chabon's literary debut at the age of twenty-four, in 1988, was heralded as the arrival of a "wonder boy" destined to be an artistic force for decades to come.

Indeed, the story surrounding publication of his first book, a bright, funny, good-natured, coming-of-age novel titled *The Mysteries of Pittsburgh*, was irresistible. Written originally as the thesis for a master of fine arts degree at the University of California, Irvine, Chabon's manuscript was submitted by a professor without his prior knowledge to a New York literary agent for consideration.

Two months later, after a spirited auction was conducted among numerous pretenders, William Morrow and Co. bought the rights to the book for $155,000, at that time a record amount for a first novel.

The book's publication was attended with considerable fanfare. Wonderful reviews, spirited sales, and a prolonged appearance on the *New York Times* bestseller list identified the young writer as one of the newly anointed, a whiz kid who had emerged among a new breed of "brat pack" phenomenons that included Bret Easton Ellis, Jay McInerney, and Tama Janowitz.

Unlike those glitzier contemporaries, however, Chabon (a Belorussian name pronounced SHAY-bahn) avoided controversy, professed a genuine work ethic, and demonstrated a healthy disdain for cocktail parties and pursuing the good life among the Manhattan elite. "I was very lucky that my entry to the literary world was through Irvine, California, and not New York City," Chabon said.

In due course, *A Model World and Other Stories*, a collection of short fiction, appeared, and growing legions of fans eagerly awaited release of Chabon's second novel.

"I felt enormous pressure to top my first novel," he admitted. "I wasn't really ready for all this attention, and I began to feel very shaky about myself and work. The truth is that I had a lot of doubts about whether I could really do another novel again."

After four years of unremitting work on a novel about an architect's scheme to create a perfect baseball park, Chabon abruptly put the 700-page manuscript in a box and tossed it in a closet. "Nothing at all felt right about it," he said. "I didn't like the storylines, I didn't like the characters, I didn't like the dialogue very much. It was just too much for me to handle, so I chucked it and turned to what was comfortable."

What was comfortable was Pittsburgh, the city where he lived for four years while an undergraduate at the University of Pittsburgh, and where he set the action of his debut work, *The Mysteries of Pittsburgh*.

From the outset of the new project, Chabon was at ease. "Within the first page and a half, I sensed I was onto a voice that I could stay with and never let me down. I don't know where it came from or how I knew what the character was going to sound like, but I found that I did, and I just climbed up on his voice and surfed."

It helped, of course, that the subject Chabon chose to develop in the new novel involved a promising young writer's attempt to produce a smashing successor to his first work. Even the title, *Wonder Boys*, had a familiar echo, and when it finally appeared last year in hardcover, the response was overwhelmingly positive.

"Chabon leaves no doubt that he is the young star of American letters," enthused Jonathan Yardley of *The Washington Post*. "Michael

Chabon can write like a magical spider, effortlessly spinning out elaborate webs of words that ensnare the reader with their beauty and style," wrote Michiko Kakutani of the *New York Times*.

In paperback, *Wonder Boys* is doing especially well on college campuses among younger readers, although Chabon's audience apparently encompasses many demographic lines. Like *The Mysteries of Pittsburgh*, it is told by a first-person narrator, but unlike the first novel, the character is older than the author, and more experienced in the frustrations of real life.

Grady Tripp, the narrator, is the thrice-married philandering author of three successful novels who suddenly finds himself overwhelmed by "what purported to be my fourth novel," a work titled *Wonder Boys*, which was hopelessly overdue and not likely to be completed any time soon.

Seeking solace from his editor and best friend from college, Grady embarks on an hilariously surreal weekend odyssey through the city of Pittsburgh that involves an array of extraordinary adventures and a panoply of incredible characters, each more dazzling than the other.

"Grady Tripp was such an act of impersonation for me," Chabon said. "I think the humor of Grady arises out of his own self and his willingness to hold himself up as an object of ridicule."

The Mysteries of Pittsburgh, by contrast, chronicles a gay love affair with such authenticity that when it was released eight years ago, *Newsweek* magazine proclaimed Chabon as one of the brightest new gay writers to appear on the literary scene.

"I was honored by the compliment, to tell you the truth, because I am very comfortable among gay people—except that I am straight," Chabon recalled with a laugh. He is pleased to point out that he is an excellent chef and that he does all the cooking at home for his wife, a Los Angeles lawyer, and their sixteen-month-old daughter.

Chabon said he is ideally suited for the role of house-husband, since his prime writing hours are from 10 P.M. to 3 A.M., leaving the days free for domestic duties. An avid collector of comic books, he is now working on a novel set in Manhattan that will focus on the golden age of the comic book.

"I see myself as a very traditional kind of writer in the sense that the conventions I write about are the conventions of another time," Chabon said. "I'm not trying any kind of bold experimentation. I'm not performing surgery on the English language."

Tom Clancy

*Interviewed in Washington, D.C.,
on August 9, 1988, for* The Cardinal of the Kremlin.

There is no way to be sure, but the release of Tom Clancy's fourth novel may mark something of a minor milestone in publishing. The man has never worked for the government, and the books he writes are fiction, yet his latest blockbuster, *The Cardinal of the Kremlin*, underwent a security review by the Central Intelligence Agency before it was submitted to G. P. Putnam's.

"The agency found out what I was working on. They asked me if they could look at it before it was published, and I agreed," Clancy said in an interview last week. "I did it on one condition, that if they wanted me to take anything out, they would have to explain why."

Clancy said he had "two guys from the agency in my house" who said they felt the material he had obtained to describe a secret Soviet research facility was classified information. "But I did not get my satellite photographs from the government," he recalled pointing out to them. "It turned out they didn't know how good commercially available satellite photography is, and if I can get it, anyone can get it, so it shouldn't be classified."

Millions of people read Clancy's books as much for the gee-whiz gadgetry as they do for the stories, and one of the attractions is the extraordinary accuracy he gives his books. He has his contacts in the military, he acknowledges, but everything he uses, he insists, is drawn from non-classified sources in the public domain.

"First and foremost, I am in the entertainment business," he said. "My job is to tell a story, but when an author is writing about topics that are current, he has a responsibility to discuss them as accurately as possible. I have reason to believe I have done this."

Stealth fighters, Yankee-class Soviet submarines, Russian Backfire bombers, Sparrow missiles, Aegis radar systems, KH-14 spy satellites, laser weaponry, and high-energy projection systems—the full load—have functions in his books, and while they are as interesting and important to the plots as the characters themselves, Clancy maintains "it's just window dressing" to the main task, which is to write about people in conflict.

Beyond his knowledge of the weapons is the hard part: the ways they are used, the tactics that are employed. How ships and troops are deployed, how air attacks are marshaled, how a modern submarine lines targets up for the kill, and how shoulder-held Stinger missiles are used to destroy Russian warplanes are among the many techniques he uses in his stories. Indeed, Clancy shared royalties for *Red Storm Rising* with Larry Bond, a former intelligence officer who used to develop war games for the Navy and helped with the scenario for a conventionally fought World War III.

The Cardinal of the Kremlin is as current as you can get, with the United States and the Soviet Union racing to see who develops deployable Star Wars technology first. The title refers to Colonel Mikhail Semyonovich Filitov, a character who made an important appearance in Clancy's first book, *The Hunt for Red October*.

Called Misha by his friends, Filitov is a highly decorated army hero who holds a key position in the Soviet military. He also is a "mole" of long standing, an exquisitely placed "asset" so valuable to the United States that his identity—even his code-name, Cardinal—is known only to a handful of Americans.

In his haste to get some important information out, Misha's cover is compromised, and it is only a matter of time before his treason is exposed. But the information he has to pass on—just what the Russians are doing with laser technology at Dushanbe, their remote base in the mountains just one hundred miles from Afghanistan—is unusually critical.

Will the information reach the West? Will Misha be brought in from the cold before he is caught? A thrilling story unfolds, one that will not disappoint any of Clancy's fans. Equally impressive is the quality of his characters; they are getting better and more credibly human all the time.

One of Clancy's central premises is that the Soviets—despite all their official protestations to the contrary—are working just as assiduously on space-based anti-missile systems as the United States is pursuing the Strategic Defense Initiative. "I have reason to believe this is the truth," he asserted. "I can show you the satellite photos."

Clancy's books are unusually popular among professional military people, and it has been suggested that he gets a lot of information "leaked" to him with the hope that he will use it in his books to promote pet programs. This the author denies.

"I find that deeply offensive," he said. "Nobody guides me in the things I write about. If someone gives me classified information, that's against the law. And the suggestion that I would use classified information for commercial purposes, that really ticks me off. It impugns my intellectual credibility. It is true that people feed me clues, and it is true that I know things I shouldn't know. But half of those things I just figure out for myself."

Clancy is pleased, though, that people in the military consider his books uncommonly authentic. "*Red Storm Rising* is required reading at the Naval War College," he said with obvious pride. "And I have lectured at the Pentagon."

The author's alter-ego, Jack Ryan—the key character in *The Hunt for Red October* and *Patriot Games*—is back in *The Cardinal of the Kremlin*, and his presence there is at the heart of a civil suit brought by Clancy's former publisher. The Naval Institute Press, which published the first novel, has brought suit claiming it—and not Clancy—"owns" the character. The suit is scheduled for arbitration, and Clancy is confident he will win.

"They've gone lawyer-happy," he said. "Hey, I gave them a chance at *Red Storm Rising* for 20 percent less than I was offered by Putnam, and they turned it down. They've got no gripe whatsoever, and they will lose big. I've offered them a settlement that will allow them to save face. If they're smart, they'll take it."

Author's note: Clancy and the Naval Institute Press settled out of court. The terms were not made public.

Walter Cronkite

Interviewed in Boston on January 28, 1997, for A Reporter's Life.

What do you miss the most now that you're retired from anchoring the news?

I miss editing. I miss being on the desk every day. I loved being a managing editor. I loved taking the news off of the wire from my correspondents, watching the stories, getting people on them, getting them done right, and editing the copy. I also like daily journalism. I would be very unhappy if I were frozen on a newspaper desk somewhere and didn't get out at all. I certainly would be unhappy being an anchorman and never getting out on an occasional story. I do have a feeling that anchor people are overused today on breaking stories. I feel an awful lot of that is show boating, big footing.

Do you feel that perhaps many of these people today are not real reporters?

Well, not the network guys. Those three fellows are all damn fine reporters. They did their apprenticeships. Dan Rather, Tom Brokaw, Peter Jennings, they are all very good reporters. And not only very good reporters, but very good extemporaneous broadcasters once they have done their reporting. I think they are very good.

But they do not have the opportunity to report like newspaper people do, to really dig deep, to write deep. That's the real thing that differentiates, I think, broadcasters from the print journalists, is that the print journalist still is capable of putting together a thousand-word story, and even much longer, on a real breaking story. That is an extremely difficult task. It requires an awful lot of organizational skill, keeping a lot of things in mind. The whole idea, as you know only too well, the idea of knowing how you progress through a story to get all those facts in, and play them at the proper point in the story, and knowing what the lead is, and then the whole inverted pyramid idea, I think, has been almost lost to print, and it never was there in broadcast journalism.

The skills of a good print reporter atrophy almost instantly when they get into broadcasting. It happened to me to a degree. It happened to every writer I tried to bring from a press service over to my news desk. I wanted press-service people, people who were fast and accurate. I wanted people who were not going to write fancy stories, but could get the facts out quickly, and I wanted people who understood the press-service business so they would not assume that every press-service story was like the word from God. I wanted them to question the press-service story when they came in. Having worked with a press service for eleven years, I know personally that we make mistakes and miss the lead. I wanted people who were going to read all thirty-eight paragraphs and say, "Wait a minute, the lead is down here."

We could be two news cycles ahead on the evening news—and were because of me mostly. That is one of the rare areas where I claim dominance. I was absolutely terrific at that. Our main wire all day was the day wire, and I said we don't write off the day wire, we don't even write the leads off the night wire, which are just beginning to come in. We have to look through that and we have got to write the overnight story, that's the story for the next afternoon. That's the way it's done on a press service, and there's no reason why we can't do it here in the news room.

You are talking here about breaking news, of course?

I am talking about breaking news.

Because with features, I can usually tell what the feature stories will be on the networks five days from now by reading the New York Times.

Of course you can.

I read somewhere that this book of yours, A Reporter's Life, **has been under contract for twenty years or so. Is that true? I guess what I'm driving at, do you feel you need to have the pressure of a deadline to get you going on a story?**

That's a good part of it. At one point I did have a deadline for this book, but I overran it by a couple of years. The story of the contract for this book is one of utter disinterest on my part and major sloth. A good friend of mine was a vice president at Knopf, Tony Schulte. Tony Schulte took my kids with his kids, and we met and had family dinners. Tony started nagging me to write a book. This was back in the Sixties, and he started nagging me that I should write a book. I said, "I have no interest in writing a book. I'm not going to write a book." He nagged, nagged, nagged, every Sunday night when we met. One evening, we might have had a couple of martinis by that time when I said, "Tony, I'll make a deal with you. I will promise you that Knopf can have my memoirs if I ever write them, if you can promise me that nobody at Knopf will ever mention this to me again. I want no advance payment. I don't want anything hanging over my head."

You didn't take an advance on this?

No, no. I said no advance payment and a promise that you will get the book, but you've got to promise me that nobody ever mentions this to me again. This was about 1972. And nobody at Knopf ever did. We made this deal over the dinner table with a handshake. I thought that was a joke, I didn't even think about it.

The next morning my agent, who is never known to have gotten up before 10:30 in the morning, called me. He called me at 9:30, and I knew it was a major crisis that he called at 9:30. He said, "Walter,

Walter, what's this about you're writing a book." He knew Tony Schulte, also, as I did. I said, "I'm not writing a book. What do you mean?" He said, "Tony Schulte thinks you are. He's just been on the phone with me, and he's got the contract drawn and wants to meet us for lunch." So we met at lunch and sure enough he had a contract saying just what I had specified. He had it in there that nobody at Knopf could ever mention it to me. And there was no deadline. The way it was phrased: If I ever wrote a book of memoirs, Knopf could have it. And also it was specified that the payment from Knopf in advance was one dollar and other considerations.

So we left and when I got back to my office there already was a call from Tony. A lawyer had turned down the contract. They said that one dollar was not adequate consideration, and therefore it would never hold up in court. I said, "Well then, there is no deal. I don't want any money hanging over my head to write a book."

He said, "Wait a minute, wait a minute. It's only ten thousand dollars." I said definitely no deal. He said, "Walter...." I said, "If I don't write the book, you're going to want ten thousand dollars back, and with interest and all of that. I'm not going to get involved with that." And he said, "Walter, you can put it in escrow." Well, I'm so dumb financially, I said, "What's escrow?" And he says, "You can put it in the bank for a specific purpose, and it doesn't draw interest, but it's always available to be withdrawn." So I said, "Well, I'll do that, that's okay." So I called up my agent and said, "I've made a different kind of deal, he's sending over the contract. I'm putting it in escrow. He said, "You can't do that. It doesn't draw interest." I said, "That's just the point, it doesn't draw interest." Well, anyway, that was the contract. And it lasted for eighteen years or more. But nobody at Knopf ever mentioned it to me again. I never heard from anybody. And I was perfectly happy in these circumstances. But I had a book kind of in my mind; I would write a little to myself.

About four or five years ago, one of the officials at Random House [Knopf's parent company] called and said, "Let's have lunch."

I said, "Before we have lunch, I want you to be sure that you have read that contract very carefully." He was kind of a humorless guy. He said, "Don't worry," and we went to lunch. We talked about a lot of mutual interests. He was hoping that I would bring it up. We finished lunch, we got to coffee, and he said, "Walter, would you consider that I have broken the contract, which I probably already have by bringing this up, if I said just one word?" I said, "I am so fascinated by what one word you could say that would make any difference, so say it." He said, "Write."

Well, that opened the discussion, obviously. I later signed a serious contract for a serious six-figure advance and a three-year deadline. And I ran two years over that.

Eventually, about 1991, I wrote a chapter—actually two chapters—and sent that over to Ash Green. He didn't get terribly enthusiastic. I sent it over to him, he called and said let's have lunch and talk about it. Going to lunch with your publisher in New York is apparently the only way you can do business. I prepared a little note for him. I handed him this sheet of paper on which I had written down some things, and I said, "Ash, rather than our discussing my two chapters, which might ruin our friendship and the lunch (I never had an editor edit a book before, and I don't know how you behave in these settings, but I can see myself being offended), I can see you having a lot of criticism. I think I would have some myself about these two draft chapters, so I present you with this note which you can simply—it's a simple question and answer—you can simply select one of these answers."

There were four items I had written. The first one was, "Walter these chapters are very interesting. We would like to see a few more." *B* was "We have got some very good people who have worked with our famous authors in the past." *C* was, "Walter, I think I would like to see some of your more serious chapters." *D* was something like "Walter, I don't think you understand how the publishing industry operates. It has changed since your contract was signed." Or something like that.

And how did he react to that?

His reaction was to show me a smile of affection. Ash is a dour kind of guy. He is not a laughing fellow. He took it, looked at it, folded it, put it in his pocket, and said, "Now, about those two chapters."

Did he recommend any changes in those two chapters?

Now, that was kind of part of the problem. He didn't get involved in changes. He simply said, "I think these look very good to me." I'm not sure he said very. He said, "I would like to wait until we get down into some of your later years," because I was doing it chronologically, from birth practically. He said, "I would kind of like to get to your professional career before we really get into it." I said, "I will be getting to that pretty shortly." It wasn't so encouraging that I wanted to rush back and get going at my computer, so another year passed. I just had more things to do. I really didn't get to it until I had a knee operation last January.

So what that means, apparently, is that once you got into it, you finished it rather quickly?

That is the journalist in me.

Was it fun once you got going?

Great fun. It was fun to write. It was fun to play with the words. It was fun to get the thing organized, though organization was the worst problem. One of the things that made it as fast as it was was that I had superb research help from one of my dear friends at CBS. That is invaluable, as you know, and a real time-saver. But in that material there would be some beautiful lines, really good lines. I was so tempted to use them but I was determined, I was determined that not one word of this book would be written by anybody other than me.

That was one of my questions. What if the people at Knopf had said to you, "Hey, there is this guy we know…?"

Occasionally people would say, "Why don't you dictate it, and we can fill it in, polish it up." Well, that was an insult.

There are a lot of your colleagues—younger colleagues—who don't feel that way.

Not only that, there are some who publish books, and that, I think, is distasteful. It is not that they are putting something over on everyone. It is distressing that they call themselves journalists, and they can't write their own books. What the devil? What kind of journalist is that?

Near the end of the book you write that people usually ask you whether or not you hope you made a difference. You say, surprisingly, that you did not. I wonder if you could explain that for me?

One of the worst pieces of writing in the book is there—there are some other examples—but that was a very bad piece. This has come up before, and therefore I know that it's misleading. What I meant to say is that in television journalism the only contribution I have made is perhaps in helping to pioneer a form of journalism which established a foundation, a set of principles and ethics that would live on, that I hoped would be as solid as good newspapers, with the CBSs, the ABCs, the NBCs of this world being the solid big boys in broadcasting like the *New York Times* is in publishing. And that they would perform like the *New York Times*, with responsibility and with understanding of what their place in society was, and I don't think that is so today.

I think the pioneers in ownership, the Paleys, the Sarnoffs, the Goldensons, while not perhaps entirely cognizant of their responsibility, understood it almost subconsciously, because they were forced to. They went through the early days of regulation of broadcasting, and they had to sit in hearing after hearing,

FCC meeting after FCC meeting, on what the responsibilities of broadcasters are. Now the FCC has, of course, totally abandoned any suggestion that it would regulate responsibility among broadcasters. But in those days, they were very serious about it. You know, for many years radio couldn't editorialize, for instance. For a station license you had to show fairness in the community, as you still have to today, although it is not in force much anymore. So those guys learned there was a responsibility in the business. Now, let me be clear: I am not talking about the journalists.

But there has been perceived to be a decline in the quality of broadcast journalism, hasn't there?

Of course, the networks are seriously culpable. They let their O and Os [owned and operated stations] put their tabloid stuff where the news ought to be. They can't control what the other stations do in the way they control what their own stations can do. As it is, they let their evening news programs go on at fringe time, and then they put in these tabloid shows at prime time. The audience is much bigger at 7:00 and 7:30 than it is at 6:30.

For those of us who grew up with Walter Cronkite, when we think of all the major stories of our time, we identify them with you, and I wouldn't ask you to pick any favorites, but I wonder, are there any stories that you didn't cover that you wish you had?

Every one that I missed.

You don't seem to show any anxiety about having missed the recent political conventions.

Well, I have had anxiety about missing them. I hate to miss them, but I don't have any outlet for my work. I have permitted myself to live under an exclusive contract with CBS all these years instead of breaking and going elsewhere. I had a kind of a loyalty. They haven't assigned me to these stories, so I am not going to go out there. I suppose I could do a newspaper column, but that doesn't interest me.

Would you say that a defining moment in your career was when you decided to make a statement of opinion about the Vietnam War?

Defining I think may be a little too strong a word. It was certainly unique, rather than defining. We didn't pursue that as an idea that I should do it. It was certainly a major and traumatic departure from what we had always done, from what I had always done, and television generally. People didn't step out of their roles in those days and do editorial comment. I only violated the role three or four times, and it was always clearly labeled as such. It always followed a commercial break so that we could say beforehand, when I come back, I shall have a personal opinion on this period, and then when we came back from the commercial break, I would say this is my personal opinion. And the only other times—other than the Vietnam War—were twice, on what I would call freedom of the press issues where I had a personal philosophy that, damn it, if we didn't cover freedom of the press, who is going to? So we had to speak out in those cases.

And of course your decision to cover the Watergate story the way you did made what was, in essence, a local story for the *Washington Post* into a national story?

I'm very proud of Watergate, and I'm proud that we did Vietnam. The only problem I had with [the latter] was that the instigation was somewhat egotistical. I mean the idea that because we had a fairly loyal audience—at least an audience that believed CBS was impartial and unbiased and unprejudiced—they might therefore want to listen to my view about what this complicated thing was all about, that was egotistical. But Watergate was not tinged with that, nor was a story of a different nature, which was the serendipity of the Sadat-Begin thing, and that was purely serendipitous. I was not playing diplomat [when I asked Egyptian president Anwar Sadat if he would meet with Israeli prime minister Menachem Begin in 1977],

I was not raising trial balloons. I was trying to knock down the story, and it just happened that because I used some good journalistic enterprise in pinning him down, and when I was startled to find out that he meant he would like to go, then I didn't let it go at that. I pinned him down to when he could go, and it turns out that that accelerated the process, which might have happened anyway. But it also might have stalled for months or years. I was very proud of that one.

Any regrets? Any stories that you feel you should have handled differently, or better?

Oh, almost daily. Almost daily. One of the worst was the one that I will go to my grave regretting. It was a story about Ham Jordan, [President Jimmy] Carter's assistant. Ham then had been kind of the scapegoat of the—well, no, that's not it—he'd been the focus of a lot of kind of critical, snide, column-type items in Washington. You remember, there was an incident in a bar where he turned over a drink on a lady or something of the kind, and then there were some suggestions that there were some narcotics involved. Well, one time Mike Wallace came back from the West Coast with a story that he had uncovered out there that Ham Jordan, according to his story—an alleged story—that Ham Jordan had been involved in helping supply cocaine at a Hollywood party. And Mike said they weren't going to use it for *60 Minutes* and did we want it for the *Evening News*? Well, yeah, I wanted the story for the *Evening News*, and we got Mike to help us pursue it, and we came up with a fairly substantial story; no proof, but enough of a substantial story to go with it. But I then yielded to the suggestion of our producer at the time that we lead with it. An awful, awful mistake. It put an emphasis on a story that it did not deserve. It put a credibility on a story which it did not deserve and did Ham Jordan a great injustice. I will say this, Ham Jordan never called me about it. I didn't hear from anybody at the White House about it. And that was worse.

If they'd called and screamed and hollered, I could have screamed and hollered back. But as it was, I felt that they had simply said, "Well, we can write him off."

Louise Erdrich

Interviewed in Boston on April 26, 1996, for Tales of Burning Love.

Whether she's "on the reservation," as she was in such bestselling works as *Love Medicine, The Beet Queen, Tracks,* and *The Bingo Palace,* or "off," as she is in her latest effort, *Tales of Burning Love,* the Native American author Louise Erdrich insists that everything she writes is all part of one big novel.

At first glance, *Tales of Burning Love* has only a passing connection with the unforgettable characters of the North Dakota plains that Erdrich has brought so vividly to life over the past twelve years in a beguiling quartet of intricately related stories.

Indeed, the very premise of the new book—four ex-wives of a purportedly deceased charmer named Jack Mauser meet up at his "funeral" and bond with tales of impossible love while stranded in a Ford Explorer during a vicious blizzard—is almost farcical in concept. Yet, somehow, through the magic of good humor, lyrical imagery, and clever storytelling, it works, and the connections with Erdrich's distinctive world become clearer.

"The truth is that I thought this book would not be related at all to the others until I was about three-quarters of the way through writing it," Erdrich confided in a recent Boston interview. Since alert readers will note an important connection between *Love Medicine* (1984), her first novel, and *Tales of Burning Love,* her latest, on the opening pages of each, a bit of explanation is appropriate.

"What happened is that I started writing this book in the middle," she explained. "I had this image of several women playing blackjack, and then I saw them trapped together in a car in a blizzard, which is not so unusual an occurrence in North Dakota. Things like that happen there all the time."

The decision to start writing in the middle, continue toward the resolution, and then swing back to the beginning, she added, developed out of a renewed fascination she had discovered for music.

"I began to take piano lessons after twenty-three years of being away from it, and my teacher suggested that I master the end of some tricky songs first. That way, she told me, you're going to give a lot more energy to your beginning when you go back and pick it up. I did that, it worked out nicely, and I thought I'd try the same technique with a novel I'd been playing with off and on for the past fifteen years."

So, with loose echoes of Boccaccio and Chaucer, what she had, in essence, was an intriguing novel involving a group of story-telling travelers, in this case four women forced by circumstance to talk about the man to whom they each had been married.

Jack Mauser is a new name in Erdrich's world, but the details of his first "marriage" in a barroom ceremony to June Kashpaw, a long-legged Chippewa woman "aged hard in every way except how she moved," will be familiar. What readers of the first book know is that after spending some time in the front seat of the man's car, June walked off into a snowstorm and froze to death. The man she had been with that night was known to her only as Andy.

June's death was the opening scene in *Love Medicine*, and it begins *Tales of Burning Love* as well, only this time we know the man's name is not Andy at all, but Jack Mauser—a man, it turns out, who has been tormented by June's death for fifteen years.

Despite being a thorough knave and irrepressible philanderer, Jack has a sense of humanity that endears him in subsequent matches with Eleanor, Candice, Marlis, and Dot, the women who find themselves sharing their "tales of burning love" while trying to stay warm in the stranded van.

"I was writing about this guy Jack Mauser, and then eventually it occurred to me that something had to have happened to throw him into this relentless search for union," Erdrich said.

"Finally, I saw him there in that bar, and I suddenly realized that June was his very first wife, married to him by a matchbook preacher in an impromptu wedding. After Jack allows June to walk off into the snow, he never sees her again, and he freezes emotionally, and for the next fifteen years he's haunted, paralyzed, and unable to bear the depth of his own feelings. So okay, he's a jerk, but at least he cares; he has basic decency."

This attitude of moderate affection for Jack is infectious, and readers will smile at his wild antics. "This is not a male-bashing book in any way, and it's not a women's buddy novel either," Erdrich said. "These women all loved him; they survived him, to be sure, and except for Eleanor, who's the most neurotic, they all outgrew him. But they don't stop loving him either."

The daughter of a German father and a full Chippewa mother, both of whom worked for the Bureau of Indian Affairs, Erdrich, forty, grew up on the Turtle Mountain Reservation, in North Dakota.

Published when she was twenty-eight, *Love Medicine* won a National Book Critics Circle Award. Especially memorable was a structure that allowed the novel to be told in seven distinctive narrative voices. *Tales of Burning Love* is of more traditional design.

"Actually hearing the voice of a character happens less and less to me as I get older as a writer," she said. "When I was a younger writer, I would always hear them as if they were talking to me. Now, I see things more and more with the omniscient perspective."

Erdrich's next novel will return firmly to the reservation, although everything is part of one larger work. "The fact is that they are all related, and it's never going to stop. If it has any shape, it's like the Great Plains; it's just this long flat road, and I'm on it for the long haul."

Robert Fagles

*Interviewed in Cambridge, Massachusetts,
on February 19, 1997, to discuss his translation of* The Odyssey.

Do you believe that every generation requires its own version of Homer, its own Dante, its own Shakespeare?

I don't think there is any question of that. Our notion of poetry always changes. Our notion of Homer is always changing. Our notion of what constitutes English poetry is always changing. But I think there is another side to that, too. Every generation needs its own translation because they are looking for the timely translation. At the same time, as you well know, there is much about Homer that is timeless, and as much as you want it to be relevant, current to your own idiom, there is another aspiration to it, too, I think, and that is to catch by contagion some of Homer's timelessness. There is always a great example behind you—Pope's Homer, Dryden's Virgil, Golding's Ovid, which were the great translations of their day, for their generation. At the same time, they were works of writing in their own right. And they lasted a good long time. Pope's Homer was Homer in England not only for his generation but for many generations afterward. And he is still read for much the same reason.

Because it became a work in its own right?

Precisely. So it is a kind of combination between timeliness and timelessness, which is what you are really after as a translator, especially when you are dealing with one of these people like Homer or Aeschylus or Sophocles, who have lingered for very good reason. They've endured for a good long time.

But on the other hand, you don't want your translation to be perceived as something that's dated to a particular time?

Not at all. You would want it read fifty or a hundred years from now. It's an immodest hope and probably an impossible one, but I think any translator in the business entertains that hope, especially when they are dealing with one of these giants, who in the case of Homer has been around for 2,700 years. You're always brought up against the question, why has he lasted so long, and if he's lasted so long, can I create something that will last a little longer than my generation?

Is English a good language for Homer to go into?

I think so. It's the only one I've got. Yes, I think there is a kind of easy flow for Homer into English, and at the same time Homer has a highly inflected language, and we don't. But Homer lends himself to hexameters and we lend ourselves more to iambics, so there are really cultural differences between the two languages. I think, in fact, that one of the interesting parts of translation is how you can stretch your own language by virtue of coming into contact with something that is as enormous as Homer. It is not only that you want to bring him into your own idiom. You want to stretch your own idiom at the same time. I think these things are always two-way streets.

You maintain that you are not a line-by-line translator; perhaps you could expand a bit on that?

Well, it is a curious combination, I think, of trying to get over into one's English line as much of what Homer says as possible, at the same time creating an English line. And the two are not necessarily perfect fits. There are times when a line of Homer will come right over into a line of English. Other times when you might even find your English briefer. I spend about as much time reading modern English literature as I do reading ancient Greek literature. I think it's a dual responsibility. It's pleasurable, but I think it's a professional necessity. Jimmy Merrill said that any writer who does not read fine modern writing is indulging in a high-risk activity. And I think it's true.

One of your reviewers has suggested that the Odyssey has supplanted the Iliad. Do you agree with that?

Not for me it hasn't. And I think, especially in our time, coming out of the Cold War and the post–Cold War readjustments, I think the so-called poem of war, the Iliad, has as much bearing on our sensibility as the so-called poem of peace, the Odyssey, remembering also that there are many tender moments in the Iliad, and there are many brutal moments in the Odyssey.

The critic Gary Wills seems quite taken by your attitude toward women. Is this something again you mindfully pursued?

I don't really think so. I think it is in Homer. I don't think that the great works of feminist criticism aren't of relevance because they are. But I think it is a question of confirmation and reinforcement, rather than pointing out things that people who read Homer deeply have never seen before.

Is this a politically correct Odyssey? And does a book have to be relevant in order to be read?

I have very mixed feelings about that. On one hand, a poem like the Odyssey is relevant. Shakespeare is relevant. At the same time Shakespeare and Homer are infinitely larger than what is relevant to our times. Maybe I can put it personally. What drew me to translate the Odyssey, for instance, was Odysseus seeing his dead mother in the underworld. That was the first thing I translated. When my mother died, I had to put together a service. Twenty years ago, I translated that part for the first time. The reunion with Odysseus and his father in the orchard in the last book—it is a painful, tortured kind of relationship that has a lot of love and tenderness to it. I enjoyed and endured something of the same thing with my father. The aspect of coming of age, Telemachus parenting Odysseus and Penelope, these are personal tugs, personal points of reference that draw me as they would draw anyone else into the poem. Relevance.

But once you're in the poem, those things are expanding 10,000 times. They become epic in their consequences, they become memorable in the poetic expression. So if it's relevance that pulls you into the poem, it's the thread of the poem, the size of the poem that expands those personal points of reference a hundredfold beyond personal experience. Two things, then: It's relevance on the one hand and great enlargement on the other.

How did you feel when you heard in the news recently that Amherst College, your alma mater, gave an English major a degree, summa cum laude, without ever having been required to study Shakespeare, Milton, Chaucer, or Spenser?

I have been concerned by such stories. Especially about a story involving Amherst, where I went to college. I would like to ask a sneaky question, however. Did that person not read Shakespeare? Do we know that? What I am getting at is this: I checked with some colleagues in the English department at Princeton, and Shakespeare is not required in the Princeton English department. Is Shakespeare taught? Yes. Is Shakespeare enrolled well? Very well, and enrollments are rising. Is Homer required? Not exactly. But is Homer read? Absolutely. What I am getting at is something very simple, I think. Phyllis Franklin, the executive director at the Modern Language Association, said it best: Something does not have to be required in order to be read. These things, Shakespeare, Homer, they are too good to go away. Simply because something is not required does not mean that it is not being taught in courses. These things are too large, too old, too good just to go away. I sense at my own university, at least, increasing interest, not decreasing interest.

There is a decrease in the number of times such things are required, but an increase in the general interest, the level of interest they arouse. Look at the sales of *The Iliad* and *The Odyssey*, for example. That is amazing. That is the most heartening thing I can imagine. These are trade book sales. It is enormously satisfying because it means that people are reading not just for recreation but to re-create themselves in some way, that there is a real hunger for something they can sink their teeth into and get some nourishment.

Is it possible that when teachers such as yourself have retired that there will not be anyone new to teach the classics?

I am not sure of that at all. Not with that much reading going on. I really mean it. I think also that we ought to have a healthier regard for some of the shifts in media. What I mean by that, *The Odyssey* is done on a wonderful audio book by Ian McKellen, and he is a superb actor. Well that has caught on very briskly. That is selling at the ratio of one tape for every five books. The usual ratio is one tape per every ten or twenty. This is part of the Shakespeare revival, I think. It is part of the great cinematic revival, things like Shakespeare, Jane Austen, E. M. Forster, Henry James. In other words it isn't simply a book culture, it is a culture that has a lot of interest in performance, a lot of interest in the visual, and we may have to shift our notions of how we approach things, how we suck the nourishment out of them. But first and foremost, they are books, and they enjoy a very wide currency.

When you say book culture, what do you mean?

You know, I am not sure anymore. When Penguin decided to put out a tape of *The Iliad* with Derek Jacobi, I thought this would be maybe interesting, but I was really afraid that such things would cannibalize the book not only in terms of sales, but that it would appeal more to the ear than the eye. And then I caught myself, and I said, "Look, Homer was performed, and if you don't have an appetite for Homer in performance, then you are not doing your job." I have been giving readings, and I don't think that book culture is just a question of people sitting in their private studies reading to themselves silently. There comes upon us a whole performative aspect because we find in the audio book, in television, in film adaptations, in the musical scores, that there is a great expansion of how old masterpieces of print and word are being absorbed and received. I don't think it's only books anymore, even though the efflorescence of libraries is something extraordinary.

Do you have any anxiety about the future of the book as we know it?

I don't think you can ever bank on anything. But I derive great heart from the proliferation of large bookstores, the amount of reading going on in the lay public. With all of that happening, I worry less whenever books are destroyed. I'm just talking about the extraordinary buoyancy, it seems to me, in the public imagination these days. And you can imagine how many of all those new children's books being sold are, in a sense, performed by parents with children. The linguistic aspect, to me that is where the power lies.

Could you talk about Homer in performance?

That is very important to me. That is something I always felt. Ever since people taught me how to speak Homer's lines. This seemed to me to be a public activity. This is not just something that we should be reading. It is a performing activity. We should be hearing, if only in our middle ear. Pope said this best, that Homer makes us hearers, and Virgil leaves us readers. This was Pope in his preface to the Iliad.

How about translations that you are thinking about working on now?

I don't know. I have been hanging out with Homer now for twenty years, and I am weary and suffering from word overload. But I also am bereft. That companionship is still with me, but it is not something I confront every morning when I wake up, and I don't really know where to turn.

Is it the companionship of Homer, or the companionship of the text?

All those things. All those things. I don't mean to be mawkish, but there is a great loneliness that sweeps over me, which my wife knows all about.

Do you think that Homer was a blind person? I know this is one of those apocryphal details, but it is still quite powerful.

It is apocryphal but compelling that he should be blind and have so much insight. We don't know where he was born, but seven cities claim him as their son. We don't know what his name meant, either. Homeros, captive—captive of the wars, or was he a knockabout, and a drifter and a performer, and therefore dependent and even hostage to the kindness of strangers? Who knows?

Penelope Fitzgerald

Interviewed in London on March 15, 1998, for The Blue Flower.

The idea of being a "late bloomer" is not a concept Penelope Fitzgerald spends much time considering, despite the fact that the eighty-one-year-old British author has become the toast of the world's literary circles—twenty years after publishing her first novel.

Widely admired as a consummate stylist with an exquisite sense of nuance, a sharp eye for detail, and a perceptive grasp of the human soul, Fitzgerald has been a finalist four times for the Booker Prize in England, winning once for *Offshore*. That novel was inspired by her own experience of having lived among a community of houseboat dwellers on a barge at Battersea Reach on the River Thames.

On March 24, Fitzgerald was the surprise winner of the National Book Critics Circle (NBCC) Award for *The Blue Flower*, a brilliantly conceived historical novel based on the early years of the German Romantic poet Friedrich Leopold von Hardenberg (1772–1801), later known by the pseudonym Novalis. The book was published in England in 1995, but released in the United States last year.

Fitzgerald is the first foreign author to receive the NBCC citation, a circumstance made possible by a new rule that allows consideration of works written by non-U.S. citizens. With Don DeLillo, Philip Roth, and Charles Frazier as her principal competition, Fitzgerald was considered a long-shot at best.

"I never anticipated anything like this," she said during a recent interview of the attention she has been receiving for her work, speaking with the same concision of thought and economy of language that characterize her writing.

We met on a drizzly Sunday afternoon at tea-time in her small but comfortable flat, a converted coach house that adjoins the late Victorian home of a daughter and son-in-law in the Highgate section of North London; she has two other adult children, a son and another daughter, and nine grandchildren. Her husband, Desmond Fitzgerald, died in 1976.

A stately, elegant woman of quiet demeanor who speaks in precisely phrased sentences, Fitzgerald does not disguise her conviction that writing is an extremely difficult and demanding exercise, something she enjoys far more for having done, than doing on a daily basis.

"It would have been nice to be a young novelist and to have developed my literary skills over a period of years, but that just wasn't something that was meant to be," she said. "You start really from nothing—all writers do—and you simply hope for the best. But it doesn't always turn out that way."

A graduate of Somerville College at Oxford University, where she studied English, Fitzgerald is an omnivorous reader of the classics. The idea to become an author was not born out of any compulsion that she had been harboring for decades toward self-expression, but from an attempt to generate income during a particularly difficult time in her life.

"My husband was very ill, and I needed to make some money," she said. "I determined that there were only two ways by which I could do this, and that was either through teaching or writing." Since she had taught at several private schools years earlier, she decided to try her hand at writing and began with nonfiction.

Her first effort was a 1975 biography of the artist Edward Burne-Jones (1833–1898), a friend and colleague of William Morris and

Dante Gabriel Rossetti. She was motivated by the artist's design of the west window of St. Philip's Church in Birmingham, where her grandfather had once been rector.

This was followed two years later by *The Knox Brothers*, a group portrait of her father, Edmund V. Knox, for many years the editor of *Punch* magazine, and his three brothers: Dillwyn, a classicist who played a vital role in decoding German communications during both world wars; Wilfred, a high-church Anglican priest and the author of many theological works; and Ronald, a widely known Roman Catholic apologist. She also wrote a 1984 biography of the poet Charlotte Mew (1869–1928).

Fitzgerald's move to fiction developed out of an attempt to write "what I thought might be a thriller" to amuse her dying husband. The result of that effort was *The Golden Child*, a witty murder mystery set in a museum that turns on the clever breaking of a code contained in an ancient artifact, a respectful nod, as it were, to the exploits of her beloved uncle Dillwyn Knox, the cryptographer.

"My publisher thought it wasn't thrilling enough to call a thriller," she said, "so they cut the last eight chapters out and called it a mystery story. I think there were some ends left hanging as a result, but it did amuse my husband, for which I am grateful."

The five novels that followed continued to draw on personal experience, and each one was written with the idea that it could be read in one sustained sitting. *The Bookshop* tells of the good-hearted widow Florence Green's doomed effort to open a bookstore in the damp seaside town of Hardborough, a community not unlike Southwold, in Suffolk, where Fitzgerald attempted a similar undertaking.

Offshore was suggested by the time Fitzgerald and her family spent living on a barge in the Thames; the boat sank twice in bad weather. She agreed that the barge may well serve a symbolic purpose in the novel, but she leaves literary analysis to the critics. "I suppose it is a metaphor," she said, but quickly added that "the boat actually did sink, you know."

Similarly, her experiences working with the BBC during the Second World War provided the premise for *Human Voices* (1980), and her years teaching at a school for aspiring drama students occasioned the writing of *At Freddie's* (1982).

"I think most people draw from their own lives," she said. "The first novels I wrote were taken more or less from my own experience, but when you get to the end of your experiences—or rather you get to the end of what you feel comfortable writing about—you go outside, and that is what I finally did."

As a change of pace, she set her 1986 novel, *Innocence*, in Florence, Italy, during the 1950s, and *The Beginning of Spring* (1988) takes place in an English community in Moscow just prior to the outbreak of the Russian Revolution. Her latest, and quite possibly her best novel, *The Blue Flower*, is entirely a work of the imagination.

"I am very devoted to D. H. Lawrence, and I was reading a short story of his called 'The Fox,' where at the end he talks about a beautiful blue flower that is always beyond our grasp, but we can't help reaching out for it," she said. "That led me by chance to an unfinished book by this German poet we know here in England as Novalis, where a blue flower figures prominently, and then I got interested in learning something about him."

Finding a set of Friedrich von Hardenberg's collected works and letters at the London Library, Fitzgerald spent two years translating all of his correspondence from German into English and getting the raw material for her novel.

Novalis, whom Fitzgerald calls by his nickname "Fritz" in *The Blue Flower*, died at age twenty-nine. The novel centers on the poet's obsessive passion for a twelve-year-old girl named Sophie, who dies at fifteen, shortly after their engagement.

"I write only in pen and ink, and I labor over every word," Fitzgerald said. "I have made a rule for myself: I don't start until I feel I have my title, my first paragraph, and my last paragraph. I can't choose the ending as I go along. I've got to have that before I can begin to write.

"Why do most of my books end up unhappy? Because I take my cues from real life."

Richard Ford

Interviewed in Boston on June 23, 1995, for Independence Day, *which went on to win a Pulitzer Prize for fiction.*

The idea of a Southern writer not having a permanent place to call home might sound inconceivable to some critics of American literature, but that is the way Richard Ford likes it, and that is the way he has gone about creating an impressive body of work over the past twenty years.

In each of the six books that the fifty-one-year-old Mississippi native has written, setting has come almost as a consequence of where he was living at the particular moment of inspiration. *Independence Day*, his new novel, is a sequel to *The Sportswriter*, his best-known work, which was published in 1986; it takes place over a Fourth of July weekend in Haddam, New Jersey, a fictional community not unlike the college town where Ford lived while teaching at Princeton University in the late 1970s.

"Americans are always moving, and that is the nature of the country," Ford said. "Most people landed in one place and didn't like it or it didn't like them, and they got up and went someplace else. If that didn't work, they kept on going. People coming to a new place and trying to be accommodated is utterly American. For me, it's also the source of a certain kind of life drama. What I like to do is exhaust my interest in a place and then move on."

Ford's first published work, his 1976 novel *A Piece of My Heart*, was set in the Mississippi Delta region of his youth. *The Ultimate Good Luck*, which followed five years later, took place in Oaxaca, Mexico, where he and his wife Kristina had spent some time. The backdrop for *Rock Springs*, a 1987 story collection that featured a cast of down-and-out characters, and *Wildlife*, a 1990 novel, is Montana, where Ford moved in 1983 when his wife, who holds a doctorate in city planning, took a job in Missoula.

Later, when Kristina became project director for the Bureau of Governmental Research in Louisiana, they moved to New Orleans, taking up residence in their twelfth home in twenty-two years. Other stops along the way have included Dorset, Vermont, and Ann Arbor, Michigan, where the couple met in 1962 and where Ford briefly studied hotel management at the University of Michigan before deciding he would take a shot at writing.

"It was just a matter of my getting beached early in my life and not being able to do anything very well to my satisfaction," he said. "I started off wanting to write stories because I hadn't already proved to myself that I couldn't do it. I was led to it by reading having meant so much to me. I thought maybe I could do for other readers what books had done for me, which was to lift me up."

The authors whose work has meant the most to Ford include William Faulkner, Eudora Welty, and Walker Percy, three Southerners whose literary brilliance, in a way, persuaded him to set his fiction in other regions of the country.

"The reason I haven't staked out Yoknapatawpha County," he said, referring to the fictional Mississippi region created by Faulkner in his books, "is because somebody else had already staked it out so wonderfully before me. Faulkner got it so right, and likewise with Eudora and Walker. They had done everything I might have wanted to write about the South; they circled it and squared it—so I was made to get out of Mississippi."

The Sportswriter and *Independence Day* are narrated by Frank Bascombe, a self-styled survivor of the 1960s. In his first appearance, Frank was a thirty-eight-year-old newly divorced journalist and occasional writer of short stories whose most remarkable trait was the equanimity with which he accepted the vicissitudes of life.

In *Independence Day*, which takes place in 1988, five years later, Frank has left journalism and become a Realtor, a job that allows him to observe the peripatetic nature of the American psyche. Even the title of the book is unmistakably American, and it functions as a metaphor for choice and opportunity. Toward the end of the novel, Frank comments on the beauty of a summer morning and what it might hold in store: "Clearly it is a good day for a fresh start, coming or going."

The story takes place over a long holiday weekend in which Frank picks up his emotionally troubled fifteen-year-old son at the home of his ex-wife in Connecticut for a motor trip to the basketball and baseball halls of fame. Before setting off on that excursion, he shows houses to some prospective buyers, and spends an unfulfilling Friday night at the Jersey Shore with his "lady friend" of the past six months, the "blond, tall, and leggy Sally Caldwell." As usual in a Richard Ford novel, all of the characters are splendidly drawn.

Most memorable is the distinctiveness of Frank Bascombe's capricious observations, the clarity of his voice, and the leisurely pace of Ford's narrative style. A number of reviewers see Frank as something of an alter ego for Ford in much the same way that John Updike used Harry Angstrom as an expression of himself in the celebrated cycle of Rabbit novels. Ford, though, maintains otherwise.

"What simply happened is that I had Frank's voice somehow echoing around in my brain, and particularly in my notebook. I found all these notes that I had been accumulating in Frank's voice, and I started trying them out on some of the things that I was interested in quite distinct from Frank. After about a year of resisting it, I just gave in and said, 'Okay, this is what the world has given me to write about,' and I fed off of it."

Ford insists that he has no further plans for Frank, but he allows himself the option of changing his mind. "Frank is gone," he said flatly. "He's gone back in the closet, where he went when I first dispensed with him nine years ago. He could come back, but in no way that I now conceive."

Kaye Gibbons

*Interviewed in Boston on June 25, 1998,
for* On the Occasion of My Last Afternoon.

On January 3 of this year, when she was supposed to be submitting the manuscript of a new book to her editor in New York, the novelist Kaye Gibbons threw the 900 pages of text she had just finished into the trash and started again from scratch.

For the next ten weeks, the thirty-eight-year-old Raleigh, North Carolina, author wrote day and night and "just continued straight on until March 15," when a satisfactory new version was completed, she said during a recent interview.

"I threw all those pages away because I knew that this was not the best I could do. I wanted the language in this book to be very strong. I wanted the words to work as hard as they could. I slept a couple hours every three or four days. I had a real creative burst there, and I stayed with it until I was done."

The result of her marathon rewrite effort, *On the Occasion of My Last Afternoon*, was rushed into print at heroic speed, and has just been released to glowing reviews, which should come as no surprise to admirers of this celebrated perfectionist's work.

Unlike her first five books, which are family stories featuring contemporary Southern women, *On the Occasion of My Last Afternoon* is a heavily researched historical novel that begins in 1842 with the narrator, Emma Garnet Tate Lowell, recalling the day her malevolent father killed a slave on his Virginia plantation.

A rich tapestry that covers seven eventful decades in nineteenth-century American history, the novel achieves full flower as a literary work during the Civil War and Reconstruction. It is narrated in 1900, as the seventy-year-old woman approaches the end of her life.

Gibbons made her debut ten years ago with *Ellen Foster*, a contemporary classic that tells of a prepubescent girl who emerges triumphant after enduring the suicide of her mother, the brutality of an alcoholic father, and the neglect of indifferent relatives.

Winner of the Sue Kaufman Prize for First Fiction from the American Academy of Arts and Letters, *Ellen Foster* still sells three thousand copies a month in Vintage paperback, and it is required reading in high schools and colleges throughout the country. It was made into a Hallmark TV movie, which aired last December.

Also in December, Oprah Winfrey selected *Ellen Foster* and Gibbons's 1989 novel, *A Virtuous Woman*, as featured selections for her television book club, which brought thousands of new readers to her work.

But there was also a downside to the new wave of attention, one that caused unexpected anxiety for Gibbons and may even have been a factor in her decision to scrap the manuscript for *On the Occasion of My Last Afternoon* and begin anew.

"I am grateful for the Oprah selection, don't get me wrong, because it has put food on the table, but it was overwhelming. The phone rang constantly, there were hundreds of requests for appearances, and people just won't take no for an answer."

Of greater concern, however, was the pressure Gibbons began to feel that she had to produce a book that would take full advantage of all this new-found attention. And when she looked at her completed manuscript, she knew that she had barely scratched the surface.

"All the research I had done on the Civil War and the era was there. I had a book, what I didn't have yet was a story. The language was flat, the characters were stereotypical, there was no luminance, no music to it, no plot."

Readers familiar with the body of Gibbons's work know that she suffers from periods of manic depression and that her mother's mental illness and suicide provided the raw material for *Ellen Foster* and *Sights Unseen*, her 1995 novel.

"I see a psychiatrist once a week and take medication, but I still have these breakthrough episodes every so often," she said. "I wrote *Ellen Foster* in six weeks, and although I don't want people to think I write when I'm crazy, I do tend to write my best when I am in this state of illness called hypomania."

As much as she fears the condition, Gibbons said it does increase her ability to perceive things. "I see connections between disparate ideas. I'm able to block out extraneous information and get right to the core of a truth. Those 900 pages I threw away—I think I wrote them when I was too normal."

Now that the book is published, Gibbons said she is going to relax and write some nonfiction, beginning with a biography of her mother. "I just want to be a housewife for a while, but one who reads Thomas Mann in the afternoon instead of taking naps. I want to cook. My kids deserve a whole lot more than I've been giving them lately."

During the ten weeks that she was rewriting *On the Occasion of My Last Afternoon*, Gibbons said that she had the full support of her husband, Frank, and their children. She also saw her psychiatrist every day.

"My doctor would say, 'We can keep you like this, but how much longer do you need?' And I would say, 'I need three more weeks, four more weeks,' and he would adjust my medication according to how I looked, and at the end I had terrible migraines. I paid for this book. I really hope people read it. It was a real trick pulling it off."

Mikal Gilmore

Interviewed on June 3, 1994, in Chicago, for Shot in the Heart, *which went on to win a National Book Critics Circle Award in nonfiction.*

It is tempting to dismiss Mikal Gilmore's recently released personal history as yet another exercise in masochistic voyeurism, especially in these days of mounting concern throughout the country over violent crime.

He is the youngest brother, after all, of Gary Gilmore, the man who was executed in Utah seventeen years ago for having blithely murdered two innocent people for no apparent reason other than his own angst, anger, and disaffection from society.

His execution was the first in the United States in more than a decade, and it began a new wave of capital punishment that continues in many states to this day. Moreover, Gilmore's brazen attitude toward his sentence—he refused all attempts at appeal and demanded that he be killed by firing squad—captured the attention of the nation and made him a bizarre kind of anti-hero in some circles.

But *Shot in the Heart* does not exploit this dark legacy, which may explain why it took Mikal Gilmore, a writer for *Rolling Stone* magazine, so long to write it.

Instead, he has written a quietly powerful book—a meditation, in many ways—that makes no plea for pity and seeks no forgiveness or approbation for the wanton crimes of an outlaw sibling. What he does do is offer valuable insight into the forces that lead some people to make catastrophic decisions about the ways they will comport their lives.

"I realized I was carrying things around with me that I never knew I had," Gilmore said in a recent interview in Chicago, where he was attending the BookExpo America trade exhibition. "I wrote this, finally, because I am a writer, and this is a story that I felt had to be told."

The fact that Gary Gilmore's story had already been told, and told quite well by Norman Mailer in *The Executioner's Song*, was, in the end, no impediment. In fact, Mailer and Lawrence Schiller, the television producer who conducted the interviews for Mailer's book, allowed him to use more than one hundred hours of tape-recorded conversations they conducted with the principals, many of whom are now dead.

"I was surprised that they were so cooperative," Gilmore said. "I had refused to talk with them when they were working on their projects. I gave no interviews at all. But they thought I was doing something worthwhile, and they agreed to help me. I'm grateful to them for that."

One reason Mailer and Schiller were so cooperative is because *Shot in the Heart*—a title with a double meaning if ever there was one—is written from the inside looking out, not the other way around. Mikal Gilmore, as a consequence, does not replicate *Executioner's Song*—which won a Pulitzer Prize in 1979—he complements it.

The youngest of four sons, Mikal was always the kid brother, the outsider, in a family that reinforced an attitude of estrangement. "I remember loving my brothers fiercely during those times," he writes, even though they were far from ideal role models.

Because both of his parents and two of his brothers are dead—only Frank Jr. survives—primary information was difficult to find. But by following the fragmentary leads that were available, and drawing on the dark, often apocryphal, tales that were passed on within the family, he was able to pursue and document his background.

His mother, Bessie Brown Gilmore, was born in 1913 and raised as a strict Mormon by repressive parents. She ran away and almost immediately took up with Frank Gilmore, an elusive man of many moods, many aliases, and many excuses. Because so much of what became of Gary Gilmore can be traced to a tradition of family violence, the ingredients are here for melodrama.

"You were wise to go away," Bessie tells Mikal at one point, after he had moved to Los Angeles from Portland, Oregon, where he had grown up. "There is some curse that has devoured us one by one, and before long it will me too. But living so far away, maybe it will never find you."

Mikal—he adopted the unusual spelling as a teenager at the suggestion of his mother—is clear about his feelings toward Gary. "I can't tell you the tremendous anger I had for him when he killed those men, and the anger I still carry for him to this day."

Almost from the outset, Gary led a life of crime, spending about twenty years in various reform schools and penitentiaries. At one point, after his release from an Oregon prison, he was given a chance to study art.

"What he did instead was come home and ask me to buy him a gun so he could go out and commit more robberies," Gilmore, now forty-two, said. "I refused, of course, but what enraged me most of all was that he had a real opportunity to change his life, and he was about to blow it all away. Gary made a lot of rotten choices every step along the way, and what happened after that never really came as much of a surprise to me."

Living as the baby brother of a notorious killer has had its burdens, and in many ways contributed, Gilmore believes, to the severe case of clinical depression he suffered for many years. There were people who reviled him for his relationship, and others, just as surprisingly, who admired him.

"All around me I had Gary's notoriety to contend with," he writes. "I met men who wanted to know what Gary was like—men who admired what they saw as his bravado, his hardness. I met women who wanted to sleep with me because I had been close to him. I avoided these people. I would live with being Gary's brother, but I would not live with being one of his fans or supporters."

The value of *Shot in the Heart*, Gilmore believes, is the focus it sharpens on the causes of crime. "We are all responsible for what we do, and I think Gary would be saying that himself. I always thought of my book as a genealogy of violence. I wanted to examine the history. I kept looking for those moments that would have made a difference, but then I realized there were way too many of them."

As for himself, Gilmore said that while he is gratified to have discovered his family, he had chosen to live his own life.

"I don't feel obliged to live according to that cast," he said. "I'm going to sit at home and write about music and tinker with computers and toys. But I will always be the brother of a killer who faced a firing squad for his crimes. There's nothing in the world I can do to change that."

Nadine Gordimer

*Interviewed in Cambridge, Massachusetts,
on October 19, 1994, to discuss* None to Accompany Me.

Over the last forty-one years, the South African writer and Nobel Prize winner Nadine Gordimer has written twenty books dealing with such subjects as interracial love, teenage pregnancy, mother-daughter conflicts, discriminatory labor practices, and postcolonial friction.

And like Gordimer's other books, her latest, *None To Accompany Me*, a novel set in South Africa, examines a society in which race is the predominant fact of everyday life.

When Gordimer won the Nobel Prize in 1991, her homeland was still three years away from abolishing apartheid and holding a general election where all citizens were allowed to vote. How has the changing political climate affected her writing?

"It makes a big difference in my life as a human being, but it doesn't really affect me in terms of my work, because it wasn't apartheid that made me a writer, and it isn't the end of apartheid that's going to stop me," said Gordimer, seventy-one, during an interview in Cambridge, Massachusetts, where she stayed while giving a series of lectures at Harvard University.

"I don't think about my work as influential at all. I'm simply trying to understand life—why we are here, how we cope with the business of being alive, what our relationships are like...."

The fact that my books were perceived as being so political was because I lived my life in this society that was so much changed by conflict, by political conflict, which, of course, in practical terms, is human conflict."

Now, she continued, "there's this very different atmosphere at home, and there is this extraordinary determination to reconstruct, to make a normal life for people out of what was abnormal. People now have to live in a new way. It's a tremendous challenge."

Although she has been identified as a voice for moral rectitude and political change, Gordimer insists that she never writes to preach or set forth an ideological agenda. "I don't think that literature should be determinedly tendentious, because at that point it fails, and then it becomes a tract. I believe that what is tendentious in fiction should come out of the character, the place, the time.

"The main thing to me about literature is that it should be in some way illuminating, that it should tell you something about how people feel and explain something of the mystery of life."

As a girl growing up in the 1930s in a gold-mining town thirty miles outside of Johannesburg, Gordimer, the precocious daughter of an immigrant jeweler, had modest dreams of one day becoming a dancer. The thought that she might one day write books that would be read and respected throughout the world was never considered, let alone taken seriously.

"First of all, I received almost no formal education as a child, so there was little thought of my doing anything beyond what other white girls in South Africa grew up to do," she said.

"I was an energetic girl, a great show-off, and also a mimic," Gordimer recalled. "But somewhere around the age of ten it was discovered that I had a rapid heartbeat, so my dancing came to an abrupt halt."

Soon, a passion for books and learning took hold. "I have to thank my mother for this, because she read to me lots when I was small, and by the age of six I was reading by myself. I just read whatever took my fancy and had no idea of the incongruity, so by the time I was eleven, I might still be reading *The Story of Dr. Dolittle*, but I also was reading Pepys's diary and dipping into Thucydides. I owe my education to the public library."

Gordimer began writing stories as well, and when she was fifteen, a South African literary journal published her first submission, a short story. "I was quite lucky in that nobody I knew took particular notice of it," she said. "It was just Nadine amusing herself. It was not regarded as anything that could possibly lead to life's work."

Nevertheless, she continued "writing and writing and writing," publishing stories and essays in "little magazines here and there." Though barred by the lack of formal education to pursue a degree, she did attend classes informally at the University of the Witwatersrand in 1944, an experience that convinced her she had found a purpose in life.

"My life opened up. I met other writers, I met young black journalists, and I found I had more in common with these people who were writing than I had with my contemporaries back in my small town."

Her first novel, *The Lying Days*, was published in 1953, and earned immediate acclaim. Although twenty books would follow over the next forty-one years, this was the only time Gordimer wrote with a particular readership in mind. "That book was partly autobiographical, and I confess I was thinking, 'What will my mother think about this? What will the people in my little town think?' I have never given it a thought since, because I think writing for a particular reader is absolutely fatal. It just weakens a book terribly."

Gordimer's novels include *A World of Strangers*, *Occasions for Loving*, *The Late Bourgeois World*, and *A Guest of Honor*, which dealt with the African situation outside of South Africa. Three of her books have been banned in her native land: *A World of Strangers* for twelve years; *The Late Bourgeois World* for ten; and what is arguably her best-known novel, *Burger's Daughter*, for six months.

Equally adept at writing stories—her shorter work has been published in *The New Yorker*, *The Yale Review*, and elsewhere—Gordimer said the material dictates the form she will employ.

"A story comes to me sort of complete, so that I know where I'm going to begin, and I know exactly where I'm going to end," she said. "It's all there.

"A novel is much more relaxed, so that in my mind I will know where I am going to begin, and there will be certain key points that I'm going to have to reach. But how I'm going to get there, and what will happen on the way, I don't know, it's such a subconscious process. It's even difficult to say when you started thinking about it. And it changes as I write it."

Gordimer emphasized that after forty years of writing, she still ponders the mysteries of life. "If you look at most writers, they usually return to the same themes in a different way with a different set of characters," she said. "I can see that in my own work. You think that you have written all that you know about this or that, and then afterward, it's as if you walked around and saw it from the other side."

Gordimer said she may never find any answers to her questions, but she will keep searching nonetheless. "I suppose, in the end," she concluded, "that writing is my answer."

Noah Gordon

Interviewed in Boston, on February 9, 1996, for Matters of Choice.

The phrase "literary phenomenon" is used often enough in publishing to be a hardened cliché. But the strange case of the American novelist Noah Gordon, whose books have enjoyed extraordinary international success over the past nine years but have gone relatively unnoticed at home, gives the expression renewed meaning.

"It's not like I'm waiting for a big breakthrough novel over here, either," Gordon, sixty-nine, announced one morning between mouthfuls of omelette at a deli near his apartment in suburban Boston. Gordon came to discuss *Matters of Choice*, the final volume in his trilogy of historical medical novels, just out from Dutton. Propelled by good prepublication reviews and selection by the Literary Guild, the novel promises to gain wider recognition among American readers than Gordon has seen in nearly thirty years of writing.

"My first book, *The Rabbi*, was on the *New York Times* bestseller list for twenty-six weeks, in 1965," he recalled. "My next book after that, *The Death Committee*, didn't do quite as well, but it did make the *Times* list for a couple of weeks, and it did get some pretty nice reviews."

But that was thirty years ago, and *The Jerusalem Diamond*, Gordon's third book, he readily admitted, "thudded in this country" when it appeared in 1979. Gordon next "spent two years working on a spy novel, which I finally abandoned. Then I decided to draw on the things I knew best from my work as a science reporter. I wrote a medical novel, which I promptly sold to Simon & Schuster."

Titled *The Physician*, the novel appeared in 1986 and "flopped" more resoundingly than *The Jerusalem Diamond*, but it did occasion a dramatic change in Gordon's fortunes nevertheless. Gordon related the circumstances during a brisk walk back to his apartment. "I worked with Herman Gollob at S&S, the best editor I've ever met. But not long before *The Physician* was supposed to come out, he left to become editor-in-chief at Doubleday, and I became an orphan, which, let me tell you, is the worst disaster that can befall any author, bar none."

To make matters more complicated, Gordon's longtime literary agent, Patricia Schartle Myrer, retired in 1984. "I became, in effect, a double orphan, with no editor and no agent. Eugene Winick began representing me a short time afterwards, but the damage had been done. *The Physician* sold 10,000 copies at best in the States, and Joni Evans [then president of S&S trade] was only too happy to release me from my obligation for my next books."

Shortly thereafter, the German publisher Dr. Karl H. Blessing, of Droemer Knaur, looking for new titles to add to his backlist, spotted a notice in the Simon & Schuster catalogue about *The Physician*. Gordon described the events that followed with relish. "He read the book, fell in love with it, took it back to Germany, and the whole company was wild about it. They ordered 5,000 readers copies and gave one to every bookstore manager in Germany. They called it *Der Medicus*, and it just went off the charts. I had tasted this kind of success with *The Rabbi*, but it had been a long drought between, and it was a revelation."

Outside Germany, *The Physician* was translated into more than twenty languages and racked up impressive numbers in Spain, Italy, France, Brazil, and Holland, selling more than five million copies worldwide. The novel that followed in 1992, *Shaman*, recorded similar numbers, and *Matters of Choice* has sold more than 600,000 copies in Germany since its release in October. Both *Shaman* and *Matters of Choice*, moreover, were published in European editions before being released in North America, an unusual occurrence, considering that Gordon is not an expatriate writer living abroad but an American who lives and works in the United States.

Asked to explain the discrepancy between Gordon's international and domestic success, Peter Mayer, CEO of the Penguin Group and Gordon's stateside editor, pointed out that *The Physician* "touched a certain nerve in Germany," and such fame has its own momentum. "When you have a really big bestseller, you're on a roll. If an author continues to write really good books, as Noah Gordon has, he's able to develop a readership that goes on for book after book." What the Europeans appreciate in him, Mayer notes, is that "he's writing, in each and every book, a terribly readable and provocative story."

For his part, Gordon remains hopeful that American readers will rediscover his work. "At first I said to myself, 'Maybe it's just something I write, something in my psyche, that appeals to German readers.' Except that I've been wildly successful in Spain, we've got terrific figures in Brazil, bestsellerdom in Italy, and I publish in an enormous number of countries." Even that is something of an understatement. Gordon was voted novelist of the year by the readers of the Bertelsmann book club, and he won the Silver Basque Prize (in 1992 and 1995) for the best-selling book in Spain.

And nothing, he added, is more universal than concern for health and medicine, which is the focus of *The Physician*, *The Shaman*, and *Matters of Choice*, a trilogy featuring generations of a single family who have been doctors at key historical junctures over the past nine hundred years. *The Physician* profiles the eleventh-century Saxon orphan Robert Jeremy Cole, who assumes a Jewish identity so that he can study medicine at a famous teaching hospital in Persia where Christians were not admitted in the years before the Crusades. As Cole's ambition to heal is realized, the reader becomes involved in the history of several medieval cultures.

Shaman picks up the thread eight hundred years later with the adventures of Rob J. Cole, a Scottish immigrant to Boston who assists Dr. Oliver Wendell Holmes in surgery, tends wounded soldiers for the Union Army during the Civil War, then carries on the family trade in the Illinois wilderness. The events of Dr. Cole's life are recalled by his son, Shaman, also a doctor, many years after his death.

In *Matters of Choice*, Gordon takes medicine to the brink of the twenty-first century, with primary focus on healthcare issues such as unwanted pregnancy, AIDS, and bioethics. The contemporary Dr. Cole is R. J. Cole, a woman whose service at a clinic where abortions are performed leads to a tragedy in her personal life and a decision to leave a senior position with a Boston hospital for a rural practice in the Berkshires. Gordon's characterization of R. J. is sympathetic and fully developed, and his understanding of ethical questions is informed and balanced.

While maintaining that the trilogy marks the end of the Cole series, Gordon allowed that one day, "maybe when I'm ninety-eight," he may produce another installment in the family saga. "But the original design is complete," he insisted. "What I envisioned from the beginning was a kind of simplified history of medicine in fiction, to be presented through generation after generation of physicians. I chose three books because it seemed that the history of medicine could be divided into three main segments."

The Physician represents medicine as it was practiced in ancient times through the mid-1800s. *Shaman* covers the invention of anesthesia and the implementation of antiseptic procedures that revolutionized the healing arts. *Matters of Choice* reflects medicine of today, when the availability of sophisticated machinery and advanced technology comes to us with a price attached.

Born in Worcester, Massachusetts, in 1926, Gordon grew up in a traditional Jewish neighborhood on the top floor of a three-decker house "that seemed to tack before the wind." His father, an immigrant from Russia, ran a small theatrical hotel called the Gordon House, which catered to vaudeville performers, and he later owned a pawn shop. Gordon was pleased to point out that Noah Melnikoff, the maternal grandfather for whom he is named, was a bookbinder and that, as a child, he spent countless hours in the public library developing a lifelong passion for reading.

Gordon joined the Army in the waning days of the Second World War and went to Boston University afterward under the G.I. Bill, earning a B.S. degree in journalism and an M.A. in English. His thesis was a novel "not good enough to be published" but acceptable for a master's degree in creative writing. In 1951, he married Lorraine Seay, and the couple moved into an attic apartment in Brooklyn, New York. "My first job was as a junior editor in the periodicals department of Avon Publishing Co., at fifty dollars a week. We published a lot of junk in those days—science fiction, fantasy, comic books. It was a great starting job, because at the center of the comic books they inserted short stories, and to earn extra money, I used to knock these things off on the weekends. I was learning how to develop story lines."

Two years later, Gordon moved to a magazine called *Focus*, eventually becoming the managing editor. When the couple decided to go back to Massachusetts, Gordon worked four more years as a reporter for the *Worcester Telegram*. In 1959, he joined the *Boston Herald*. "I did hard news and soft news—but what I loved most of all was science and medicine. Before long, I was named science editor."

Thus began a lifelong infatuation with subjects that in time would provide the raw material for Gordon's later novels. "I covered space shots in Florida, I wrote about the development of nuclear power, I became interested in genetics, I studied experiments on glaciers in Greenland, I observed autopsies at the Harvard Medical School and, over a period of about four years, I was allowed to witness many surgeries, some of them history-making."

The sale in 1961 of a magazine article to the *Saturday Evening Post* brought Gordon in contact with Patricia Schartle, his first agent, who negotiated terms for subsequent stories and the sale of a proposal for his first novel to McGraw-Hill. "I had an idea about a young man caught between his call to the rabbinate and his love for the daughter of a Christian minister and caught, as I had been, between American worldliness and the ancient traditions of the Jewish people. Pat Schartle got me a $7,500 advance, which was pretty nice money in those days." He took a six-month leave of absence from his job and eventually left journalism permanently. While writing *The Rabbi*, he co-founded a medical journal, *Psychiatric Opinion*, and later launched the *Journal of Human Stress*. (He is no longer involved in these publications.)

For the past eighteen years, the Gordons have divided their time between their house in a small western Massachusetts town and their apartment just outside of Boston. "I love to garden, I love to fish, and I've done some serious thinking about retirement," Gordon admitted. "But during a trip to Europe last year, a Spanish businessman told me a story about how his ancestors, Jews in Spain, had been driven out of the country in the 1500s by the Inquisition and then came back two hundred years later with Catholic names. A lot of people did that, apparently, and the idea hit me immediately for a book about the Inquisition."

The book is tentatively titled *The Secret Jew*, and Gordon hopes that it will reach more American readers when it is published in several years. He now doubts he will ever retire. "What I know for sure is that I still get up every morning excited about what I'll be writing during the day. I haven't lost my creative energy, and as long as it's there, I'll keep on writing."

Donald Hall

*Interviewed in Boston on June 3, 1996, for The Old Life;
in 2006, Hall was named Poet Laureate of the United States.*

Writing at the highest levels of accomplishment has sometimes been described as a daunting process of finding excruciatingly precise words to fit unusually demanding situations. Donald Hall, a true man of letters whose passion for seemingly endless revision is legendary, not only agrees with that premise, but goes further when he is writing poetry to consider cadence, structure, and nuance, even the specific number of syllables that will appear in every line of verse.

As the calendar continues its inexorable countdown to the next millennium, and as increasingly powerful computers usher in what has been celebrated as the information age, it is instructive to examine the labors of a consummate craftsman who typically spends four or five years working on individual poems for no reason other than "getting the words right and in the proper order."

The thought of producing a completed work in the first attempt is almost laughable for Hall, whose latest collection of four highly personal poems, *The Old Life*, is a perfect case in point.

The longest poem in the book, the title poem, is a ninety-six-page narrative that embraces the full sweep of Hall's life, from his earliest memories growing up as a child some fifty-five years ago, to the death last year from leukemia of Jane Kenyon, his wife of twenty-three years and also a poet of considerable renown.

Read in a single sitting, the title poem offers what amounts to an autobiography in verse, a memoir of eventful times recalled with enviable economy of language. A close examination shows that there are fifteen syllables in every two lines of the poem, an unusual construction that Hall imposed upon himself "simply because I like the shapes I could make with it, and because it pleased me," he said.

"I don't expect anybody to ever notice this, which is why I took special pains to disguise it," he explained. "Generally, when you're working with syllables in poetry, you do it with each line, but here I took every two lines, and allowed myself to split them up at any point. So sometimes there may be lines of sevens and eights, other times there may be tens and fives but they always add up to fifteen for every two lines."

Hall said that the benefit of imposing such a rigid structure on himself is that it "helps the creative process" by making him be inventive within the guidelines he has established. "Part of the process of revision is to force you to think over every single word. So a form like that, which basically is a constraint, actually becomes a liberation, because it requires you to think every word through until every one is perfect."

This poem, like virtually every other poem he has written over the past forty years, was deemed publishable only after he had produced scores of drafts. "I write in longhand, and I have a typist who types up fresh versions for me every day. People say to me, 'How do you know when a poem is done?' I tell them, 'Well, I don't.' Because after a book comes out, I begin to make changes in the margins."

During the 1950s, Hall was poetry editor of the *Paris Review*, editing numerous anthologies that showcased the work of younger poets. A graduate of Harvard College and Oxford University, he taught at the University of Michigan for twenty years before moving into his ancestral farm at Eagle Pond, New Hampshire, with Jane Kenyon, his second wife.

In addition to the twelve volumes of poetry he has published over the past forty-one years, Hall has written many essays on subjects ranging from baseball to the sculptor Henry Moore. He also is the author of numerous children's books, including the hugely successful *Ox-Cart Man*, a story of New England farm life and the winner of a Caldecott Medal in 1980.

Now sixty-eight, Hall has survived several frightful encounters with cancer. In January 1994, his wife, nineteen years his junior, was diagnosed with leukemia. A good deal of *The Old Life* deals with grief, particularly the eight-stanza poem "Without," which is entirely devoid of capital letters and punctuation, and concludes the volume; it deals frankly with disease and the ominous prospect of imminent loss.

"It's not an especially hopeful poem," Hall agreed. "It is a poem written out of illness, not out of death. It is about how it was to live with this disease for fifteen months. I began it about six months into the disease. I'd never written a poem before that was so asyntactical and unpunctuated, but that was what I wanted at the time. It is a poem that came out of thoughts."

As a rule, Hall continued, poems do not emerge from his considered thoughts, but more subconsciously from a variety of subtle sources, seemingly forgotten experiences among them.

"That year was without seasons, without compartments, without divisions, and then I thought, without punctuation, and that of course brought me to the poem. That one probably went eighty or ninety drafts—something like that—and I read it to Jane several times along the way."

Since Kenyon's death, Hall said he has "done nothing but write poems about her," and has begun writing her "letters in verse, telling her what's happening, remembering things." Some of the letters, he added, have gone through 120 drafts, and he will continue revising until he feels they are ready for publication.

"I do this because I want to write a beautiful thing that will last forever," he said. "I'm not telling you that I believe I will do that, but that's what I want to accomplish. A beautiful thing that will last forever is directed outward. It comes from you but it goes elsewhere."

Joseph Heller

Interviewed in Boston on September 25, 1984, for God Knows.

At first, the idea was to write a love story, a novel that would be entirely different from *Catch-22*, *Something Happened*, or *Good As Gold*. "There I was, wondering what a love story would be," Joseph Heller recalled last week in his agreeable Brooklyn accent. "Then, I may have forgotten that, or it may have been bad, or it may have been one of the seeds that was planted, I can't really say for sure, but the next thing I know, I'm hearing, 'I've got the best story in the Bible.'"

It was a voice, unmistakable and clear, and the voice belonged to David, the killer of Goliath; David, the husband of Bathsheba; David, the hard-nosed king of Israel. "I can tell you exactly the first sentences that came to my mind," Heller said. "'I've got the best story in the Bible. Job, forget him. Genesis, the cosmology is for kids. Abraham's okay. Joseph's good, but he drops out kind of suddenly. Moses is not bad, he had the Ten Commandments.'"

Then, Heller said, came the crucial sentence. "'Michelangelo made statues of us both. His is better.' Now what that gave me is not only the voice and the tone, which of course is David, but also the arbitrary time structure. I know when David is saying Michelangelo made statues of me and Moses, he's looking ahead about 2,300 years, and if he can reflect on that, he can reflect on anything."

Thus, in one creative moment came the idea for an extraordinary novel, and it came intact. Before he put pencil to paper, Heller knew where he was going. "With all my novels, I get the basic idea in a flash, maybe within two or three minutes," he said. "I get a plan for the novel, not only for the subject, but the personalities. When it came to the actual writing of this novel, I did a little research, which was mainly to read the two books of Samuel twice."

God Knows is David's story, told by David on his deathbed. As with Heller's earlier work, there are moments of great poignancy balanced by moments of humor, much of it raw and ribald, some of it sneaky and subtle.

Heller's David, to put it mildly, speaks directly. Because he can see through the ages, he can talk about anything, be it Renaissance art, Shakespearean drama, the PLO, or hot pastrami sandwiches. David's first wife, Saul's daughter Michal, always is complaining and making demands. "Go take a bath," she orders him on their wedding night. "Wash under your arms. Make sure you comb your hair after you've dried it, the back of your head, too. Rinse your teeth with a mouthwash. Use a perfume on your face." An exasperated David concludes he has married a "bona-fide Jewish American Princess," "the first in the Old Testament to be stuck with one."

But like all good comic novels, *God Knows* is bittersweet, with an undercurrent of profound sadness. "The closer I come to death, the more I hate life," David says cynically. In a final, powerful scene, he has a vision of himself as a ruddy, handsome, vibrant boy with bushy locks and a voice that is clear and pure, a lad who savors life. "And I look around me for a javelin to hurl at his head."

Most of the scenes and episodes that Heller has manipulated come directly from the Old Testament. The unusual dowry Saul demands for the hand of his daughter, for instance—one hundred Philistine foreskins—is accurate. Heller's wild description of their acquisition, needless to say, is imaginary. When David is captured and brought before a Philistine king, his method of escape is to feign madness. This is drawn from the Bible as well. David's "antic disposition," which includes a shameless rendition of "Sonny Boy," is a memorable invention.

"I'm very aware I'm dealing with a narrative line that's regarded as sacred, particularly by people who don't read the Bible and know nothing about it," Heller said. "The idea of using the profane and the obscene in connection with a sense of humor is also an effort to underline the David story. But underneath it all is a tremendous amount of seriousness involved with a man growing old and watching his family deteriorate.

He maintains, however, that despite its biblical inspiration, *God Knows* is not a theological book. "I don't think of it as a religious novel, though it does raise the question," he said. "And you ask if it's a Jewish novel, I don't think so either. I have never thought of David being Jewish. I don't think of these characters as being Jewish. They are fixtures of existent myth. I suppose it's a novel about someone who is Jewish way back. But it really is a love story, a sex story, a story about growing old, a story about political ambition, a story about war, a story about everything else."

And for the first time, Heller cannot be accused of having written an autobiographical novel. "Well, it does get close to me because now I'm almost David's age. He's seventy, and I'm sixty-one."

It could be suggested, too, Heller added, that when he was seriously ill recently and admitted to the intensive care unit of Mt. Sinai Hospital in New York with a terribly debilitating disease called Guillain-Barré Syndrome, his experiences, in a way, were paralleling those of his character-in-progress.

"There I was, lying in bed, helpless and needing constant care, and I couldn't help thinking of David. But it had no influence on the book, not in the least, because I had 325 typewritten pages when I came down with this. It came on suddenly. There was no pain, just a perplexing loss of muscle power. I had the manuscript brought to me in the hospital, along with six dozen No. 2 pencils, finely sharpened, because when I get a manuscript back, I change words incessantly. The next day, though, I couldn't even lift a page, I couldn't hold a pencil. But this didn't influence the book because three or four months later, when I was able to read the pages, it looked pretty good. When I resumed the book, it was still very clear in my mind."

A fact of life Heller has had to deal with for twenty-three years—ever since the appearance of *Catch-22* and the enormous influence it has had on a generation of readers—is that he will always be identified with that book.

"How do you follow *Catch-22*?" Heller asked in response to the question. "What I did was deliberately set out to write a book that could not possibly be construed as an imitation or a sequel. *Something Happened* is almost a complete opposite. The language is very controlled; even the narrator Slocum is in possession; he feels in control. When he's under emotional stress, then the language breaks down."

There were thirteen years between *Catch-22* and *Something Happened*, an interval dictated partly by the overwhelming success of the first novel, but there also was another factor involved. "I found myself in a catch-22 situation," Heller said. "When *Something Happened* was published, a very large number of reviewers felt cheated. They were outraged and they complained about the book because it was not at all what they had expected from the man who had written *Catch-22*. Whereas, if I had written another *Catch-22*, they would have felt I was cashing in."

So what does a writer do? "I made the right choice. *Catch-22* is organized and presented in vocabulary and sentence structure that suggests disorientation, violent dislocation. *Something Happened* develops the conscience of a man and suggests over-control and over-regimentation. It's a completely different novel."

Though there are moments of great humor in all his work, *God Knows* is arguably the funniest. There are times when you think you are reading the makings of a Mel Brooks film. "I knew it was funny when I was writing it," Heller said. "There was a definite intention on my part to make it funny and to make it liberal. This intention is consistent with what I have done in my other novels, which is an attempt to combine opposites, to combine the incompatibilities."

In addition to seeing the story whole at the outset, Heller said the character of David came complete to him as well. "A man who says I've got the best story in the Bible, mine is better than the others, given those lines, the character is right there," he said. "He's competitive, he's been irritated, everything flows from that. We're talking about a modern real-estate man, also a modern author. It was good for me that David was a composer, a writer of songs. Here I could identify very closely with him. He's jealous of Shakespeare. I'm jealous of Shakespeare."

During the period between his first two novels, Heller also wrote a play, *We Bombed in New Haven*, which was introduced at the Yale Drama School and appeared briefly on Broadway.

"It was not a big hit and not a big flop," he said. "The play was an interesting experience, but I discovered I only wanted to write novels. In theater, it's the acting that transcends the quality of the writing. I enjoy the solitary nature of creating novels. I enjoy the intimacy, the privacy of working only with myself. A novel is my own."

Joseph Heller

*Interviewed in Boston on February 25, 1997,
for* Now and Then: From Coney Island to Here.

What was the motivation to write this memoir?
In this book I wanted to concentrate on those experiences that relate to my work. The relationship between me and what I have done in my novels. But I realized that I was actually writing about myself. And my own past to a large extent. Plus the fact that over the years very many people continue to ask me why I don't write something about Coney Island. And it was an absolutely wonderful place to grow up in, and I grew up there, myself and hundreds of other kids. I couldn't think of a better place to grow up, even in the absence of money or luxuries.

When writing fiction you can hide behind your characters. In the memoir do you find it more difficult?
It was a thrilling process for me. Psychoanalysis helped me understand myself. I could not remember anything about my father. When the Jewish father died, I have no memory of that from five years old. Outwardly, I was a very happy child. Internally, I am aware now of anxiety, the nail biting. I still do that. It's easier to do than to give it up.

How did *Now and Then* come about?
When I finished *Closing Time*, I had to reconcile my memory

with those characters. I had an interest in myself. The other thing is that I had no better ideas for a book than to do this. And the third thing is that the precipitating force came from Christopher Buckley, who edits a magazine for Forbes called *Forbes FYI*. We got friendly because he wrote a very nice review of *Closing Time* in the *New Yorker*, which was the first good review I ever got in the *New Yorker*. I still haven't got one in the daily *New York Times*. He wanted me to write a piece, and he suggested something that I couldn't refuse. I would go to Rome. He would send me to Rome to write a piece. To eat. I would go to Rome and go to a few restaurants and eat. And then write a piece contrasting being in Rome now and in 1944. I couldn't turn it down. I went, and I wrote a piece. I am not a food writer. I am not a gourmet. I just like to eat, and a lot of the piece had to do with my reflections, observations, and memories. I sent nine thousand words in. He could only use three thousand. So that left me with six thousand words about myself. I wrote some things about myself—about Jewish cooking—that preceded Rome, and it ended with my coming back on a naval troop ship and going back to Coney island. I had six thousand words left over, so I just picked up on that and wrote this book. I worked most of that stuff into different chapters here. I have not wasted much in my lifetime.

Why is it that people always seem so surprised when you say you think *Something Happened* is your best book?

More and more people tell me they think it is the best of my books. *Catch-22* you generally read when you are young. Everybody will try to read it at a fairly young age. *Something Happened* seems to be one that they come to later. I love *Catch-22*, but to me that is the best book.

Do you agree that *Catch-22* is a book that only could have been written at that point in your career?

Absolutely. I couldn't have written it when I was sixty, and I wouldn't have written it, because of the Vietnam War. World

War II was a war in which almost every American was involved in one way or another. In the post-war period, which was extremely troubling and disruptive to most of the country, you had the conservative right, you had anti-abortion. Many people feel very passionate about it, but most people are outside that stuff. But World War II was big and the post-war period was big. Had I written a realistic book about World War II, it would be on the shelves of libraries, maybe taught, but there would be nothing exciting or new about it. Milo Minderbinder and Major Major are everywhere. I still hear from people, and they tell me they have met all of these characters.

You do suggest in this book that certain people from your life influenced these characters.

Yes. The only one I saw after the war, Joe Chelenko, recognized aspects of his personality. He's the only one. I wonder if I had not met him if he would have recognized himself.

Have you ever given any thought to tinkering with completed work?

Never. I don't normally reread my works. I do look at parts of *Catch-22*. I am greatly impressed with the quality of my writing. I don't think I wrote it. I see descriptions, I see phrases, I see images, and I say, "Hey, this is pretty good." I see forms of literary language. When did I ever think of those words, where did I ever get that phrase? It sounds like Evelyn Waugh's description.

Where does it all come from?

It's a struggle. I want to get a page a day when I'm writing, and then move on to the next page. But it's never finished, especially since the word processor came into my life. Each time I add to it. I'll write pages in long hand, and then I'll go to the keyboard to enter it, and in entering it I change things. And each time I add, I will reread everything that's in there. And then when I print it out I'll reread it and make changes in pencil. Language is a struggle for me.

That's a pretty remarkable statement since a title that you came up with has entered the language.

And by now, I'm 75 years old. Right now I can look back and feel satisfaction in having achieved that. It makes me feel pretty good. The last few paragraphs in the book explain how I feel about this and how well things have gone for me. A few reviewers haven't liked the sense of self-satisfaction. I think they want me to be a New York intellectual, to be glum and to be profound.

Vonnegut says he is done. How about you?

I have a different attitude. It could be I'm done, but it will not be by intention. I want to keep writing for the same reason I think Vonnegut should keep writing; that is, we have nothing better to do that we enjoy more. The publication process can be agonizing, the editing process can be. I've never had that, by the way. When I finish a book, it's done.

Do reviews bother you?

I would rather not see them unless they've very good. If they're published in New York, then I see them. At any rate, I have nothing better to do.

Do you have any ideas for a new novel?

No, I don't. I never have had an idea for a novel.

Will there be a sequel?

I hope not. I don't know what else I could write about this one life that would be interesting and unusual. If there was anything unusual about the breakup of my marriage, it might be worth writing about, but there isn't. The Sunday *Times* says I don't want to talk about it. I don't want to talk about it because it's not particularly interesting.

Do you think Vonnegut will write again?

I think Vonnegut will write. He has no hobbies, I have no hobbies. If I have nothing to do with my time I get very depressed. I like to write, and I like to write difficult books.

Does humor come naturally, or do you have to work at it?

It comes naturally. If I'm not working I can get very gloomy. And the other side of me, when I relate with people, I like being with them, like you here this morning.

John Irving

*Interviewed in Dorset, Vermont,
on August 25, 1994, for* A Son of the Circus.

If any writer of serious fiction can be described as "review proof," it has to be Vermont author John Irving, whose triumphs have included *The World According to Garp* and *The Cider House Rules*. One need look no further than the fifty-two-year-old novelist's latest effort, *A Son of the Circus*, a huge, Dickensian kind of production set mostly in modern-day India, to illustrate the point. The publication date for *A Son of the Circus* was announced as last Monday, but because books were shipped to stores throughout the country well ahead of the official release date, *Circus* has been appearing on all the important bestseller lists without benefit of advance press notices or major advertisements.

So whatever the nation's critics have to say in the days and weeks ahead—and Irving has a determined corps of detractors along with his legions of devoted readers—*A Son of the Circus* will not suffer at the cash registers, a circumstance that the popular author accepts with mixed emotions.

"It disturbs me that there are people out there who are so set in their minds that to them 'literary' means 'barely known,' or 'not well known at all,'" Irving said during an interview in his spacious office, a sunny room in his secluded house that looks out on a spectacular range of the Green Mountains.

"By that reasoning, if you're a literary writer, it means you can't be on the *New York Times* bestseller list, because all bestsellers are perceived to be slick trash, commercial fiction. While that may be true a lot of the time, it is not always the case. I'm not unique. I'm not the only literary author who has bestsellers."

Irving acknowledged that a good deal of the hostility directed toward him over the years has derived from his tendency to use exaggeration as a fictive device, and his frequent use of "misfits" and "freaks" as characters.

Irving's most controversial depiction was his creation, in *The World According to Garp*, of a hard-core group of radical feminists known as the "Ellen Jamesians" who cut out their tongues as a gesture of solidarity with a mutilated rape victim. Though clearly satiric, this characterization outraged many women, and some publishing observers believe that Irving's breakthrough novel failed to win a National Book Award for this very reason.

In the works that followed, *The Hotel New Hampshire*, *The Cider House Rules*, and *A Prayer for Owen Meany*, Irving continued to present a striking variety of memorable characters and disjointed situations, some of them decidedly grotesque.

So *A Son of the Circus* marks something of a departure for Irving in that the setting is India, not New England, and Dr. Farrokh Daruwalla, the principal character, is not American, but a native of India now living as an orthopedic surgeon in Toronto.

Not surprisingly, there is a strong cast of unusual characters that includes circus dwarfs, transvestite eunuchs, transsexual prostitutes, and identical twins separated at birth—one of them an Indian movie idol, the other an American Jesuit, and both of them gay.

For all these echoes of earlier themes, Irving said that he relies on exaggeration less now than he did before. Many of the characters in this book, he said, developed from real-life observations he made during a month-long research visit to India in 1990; about half of his time there was spent traveling with an Indian circus.

"These people are largely seen through Dr. Daruwalla's eyes, and Dr. Daruwalla is the least freakish, the most ordinary of people that I've ever written about. He is, in a good sense, absolutely the most normal character I've ever created. And he looks upon these people not as freaks, but with affection."

Indeed, the reason Dr. Daruwalla, an orthopedic surgeon, returns periodically to his native country is because he is trying to find the genetic marker for achondroplasia, an actual condition that causes short-limbed dwarfism.

Achondroplastic dwarfs comprise the majority of circus clowns in India and are central figures in the novel, which is tied together by an intricate web of flashbacks and flash-forwards, and a plot that involves a bizarre series of serial murders.

Irving said the idea for the book came to him about five years ago while he and his wife were living in Toronto and returning home from dinner. "We were stopped at a red light. It was Christmastime, snow was falling, and I saw a man, a pedestrian, also waiting for the light to change, and he looked a lot as I describe Dr. Daruwalla at the end of the book."

Irving recalled being moved by how elegant the man looked, "how well-dressed, dignified, and composed he was; it struck me that whatever life he must have come from, whatever his birthplace, he could never feel entirely assimilated, and that the richness of where he came from was a very big part of his life."

That experience not only inspired what became the book's epilogue, but was the point at which Irving began the creative process. "It seems that I always begin thinking of a story at the ending, and I need to work my way back to where it begins," he said. "This is where Dr. Daruwalla finally realizes that he will always go back to India, that he will keep returning, and he's no longer kidding himself that he's doing it just for the dwarfs."

Before *The World According to Garp* became an international sensation in 1978, Irving labored for ten years as a writer of highly regarded but virtually unknown novels. His first three books—*Setting Free the Bears*, *The Water-Method Man*, and *The 158-Pound Marriage*—sold fewer than 15,000 copies combined.

Today, Irving's books are published in thirty-four languages, and half of his income, he pointed out, comes from foreign sales. "For all that, the sad fact is that in so many cases, the reader doesn't find you unless there is a good review," he said. "The reader just doesn't know who you are, and that is the case with so many writers who just aren't well enough known. They desperately need the good review, well placed and well timed, in order to get to the reader."

While Irving now gets more than his share of enthusiastic reviews, he credits his continuing success to word of mouth, not press notices. "The person who read my last novel—or any novel of mine—and loved it is going to keep coming back until I've written a couple in a row that they really hate. And that hasn't happened yet. You must understand this is very crippling to those reviewers who don't like me. They look upon me as a sort of spreading disease that can't be stopped."

In sum, the one-time wrestling coach and former instructor at the University of Iowa Writers Workshop declared himself to be "happy with the structure and seamlessness" of his latest work. "I think it's a novel that will please the people who have found elements to like in my previous books because it has more of those elements," he said matter-of-factly.

On the other hand, he cautioned, readers who "don't find the convolutions and labyrinths of my storytelling enjoyable—those who find it tedious and manipulative and difficult and who have been irritated by my books in the past—those readers will be put off even more by this one. So be it."

Kazuo Ishiguro

Interviewed in Boston on October 12, 1995, for The Unconsoled.

After writing a novel that captivated millions of readers throughout the world and became the basis for a superb motion picture starring Anthony Hopkins, the British novelist Kazuo Ishiguro knew that expectations for his next work would be almost impossible to satisfy.

"It's a fine line that you walk," the soft-spoken London resident said during an interview in Boston. His trip to the United States was occasioned by publication of *The Unconsoled*, his first book since the triumphant release of *The Remains of the Day* six years ago garnered a Booker Prize and made him an international celebrity at the age of thirty-four.

"My last book was both a commercial and critical success, which is a wonderful combination, but the result is that the pressures are quite complicated," he continued. "On the one hand, there is the pressure to produce a book that once again will appeal to a wide audience, a book that can be turned easily into a movie. On the other side is the critical success, which can make you artistically ambitious; it can encourage you to push out into territories you haven't worked before."

Ishiguro chose to explore what for him was uncharted terrain, and the critical reaction to what he produced has been decidedly mixed. Instead of using a conventional expository technique for *The*

Unconsoled, he allowed Ryder, his narrator, to enter an alternative world in what can only be described as a dreamlike state.

Some critics have called the book Kafkaesque for its almost surreal vision; others have described it as a "postmodern nightmare." Reviews in England and the United States have ranged, in Ishiguro's words, from "declaring the book to be a masterpiece to dismissing it as a monstrosity." Either way, he considers it the most important book he has attempted.

"I can't work on a book with any real passion unless it's something I'm really interested in; I can't get too excited about going over the same ground over and over again. The idea that I might be writing to satisfy the demands of some abstract market out there isn't motivation enough for me."

Having said that, Ishiguro quickly added that, unlike some authors whose skins are so thin that they refuse to read reviews of their books, he pays close attention to everything the critics have to say about his work. "Since I am trying to communicate with other people, it is important for me to see the reviews as a whole, to try and gauge what has been received by my readers."

It is mildly ironic, he added, that *The Remains of the Day* came as the result of an attempt to shed an earlier literary image. His first two books, *A Pale View of Hills* and *An Artist of the Floating World*, used a variety of Japanese characters, settings, and images to explore a number of themes. Those factors, along with Ishiguro's name and distinctive Asian features, led many observers to assume that he is an authority on Japanese history and culture. "I was born in Nagasaki, but my family moved to England when I was five years old, and I didn't go back for almost thirty years," he explained.

"I grew up in Surrey and studied philosophy and literature at the University of Kent and the University of East Anglia. I have a Scottish wife, and I am a British citizen. But every time the BBC needed an expert to go on television and comment on the yen or about some trade war breaking out between the United States and Japan, they asked me."

To prove once and for all that he knew "absolutely nothing about economics"—and that his sensibilities were largely English and just marginally Japanese—Ishiguro decided to write *The Remains of the Day*, a novel about an impeccable British butler whose short motor trip through the countryside in the summer of 1956 evokes a striking complex of memories and emotions.

"My books are all led by theme and character," Ishiguro said. "I don't ask myself what should happen in my books. I tend to think about the plot as the product of what emerges as I explore these themes and develop these characters. They always come first for me."

In the case of Ryder, the renowned classical pianist who narrates *The Unconsoled*, the stylistic device involves "an alternative to the flashback and the reassessment kind of method, which I use in *The Remains of the Day*, and indeed, an alternative to the straight chronological, biographical method."

Instead of recalling the central events of his life, Ryder divines aspects of it through confrontations he has with apparent strangers in an unnamed Eastern European city he is visiting. Ryder believes he is there to perform at a concert, but every time he meets someone, there is an unsettling release of vaguely familiar information. The action transpires in four revealing days, but the scope is one person's lifetime.

"I thought I would take a few pivotal days in somebody's life, during which time you will somehow learn about the whole of his life," Ishiguro explained. "You get memories in *The Remains of the Day*. Here, I thought, why not have him stumble into a landscape, have him bump into people whose lives and stories he appropriates to tell his own story. They are in some way echoes of himself. Only you don't know the literal facts."

Ishiguro said he is working on his next novel, and even though he hopes he has many years of productive work ahead of him, he believes now is the time to experiment. "If you're a novelist my age, you've got to really go for it. I see so many writers of my generation just treading water, waiting until they're in their fifties or sixties to write the really big books. I believe the time to hang around in nightclubs and enjoy yourself is in ten year's time. This is the time to take artistic risks."

Alfred Kazin

*Interviewed in New York City on November 5, 1997,
for* God and the American Writer.

You quote Edmund Wilson three times in this new book, God and the American Writer, **to the extent that we no longer need religion. Do you find that sentiment works perhaps as something of a counterpoint to this book?**

Did I use that three times? In this book?

No fewer than three.

I see. Well, Wilson represents—like Mencken and many other people in the 1920s, which is his real period—what I call his revolt against his father's religion. His grandfather was a Presbyterian minister, and at one point in my book I note how all the writers—Wallace Stevens, H. L. Mencken, Sinclair Lewis—of the Twenties revolt in one way or other against their father's religion. It has no relationship with anything that I believe or that is going on right now.

I see, but where you certainly are tracing the influence of religion, it is almost a counterpoint theme.

No, I told you, it is not. I said it is a personal remark. Wilson was a very cranky, very self-opinionated man who had made up his mind that we can live without religion. But that did not affect some of the writing of the Twenties. It was his own personal thing.

This book appears fifty-five years after your first book. Do you think that it is appropriate for this point in your career?

I don't know what that means.

Do you think that it is part of the continuum of your intellectual development as a literary critic?

I don't think in those terms. I don't think of my career. I don't think of what's appropriate or anything like that. A lot of my books came out of deep personal urgency, which had nothing to do with anything except my own problems or my own interests. I don't think about my career. I don't believe in careers. I wrote this book because I have had a long-standing interest in the subject over twenty years. But it has nothing to do with being appropriate to my career.

You may find this peculiar, but I don't. I'm not interested in my career. I don't believe that careers are interesting. I don't think of a work that is going to be appropriate to my career. That puzzles you, I can see that, but the fact is that's true. I didn't write this book to fill out anything. I wrote *On Native Grounds* and published it in 1942 because that was the time to write it for me. *For me*. I don't look around and say the country needs a book like this. Do you understand?

Yes, sir.

What I say is that I want to write a book like this for myself. All of my books come out of my deep personal interests.

You mention in the book that Melville was transformed by reading Hawthorne. I love that word, *transformed*. Have you ever been transformed by reading anyone?

Of course. I'm constantly transformed by books. The word transform is exactly what I go through when I read all sorts of things, when I reread *Moby-Dick*, which I edited many years ago. I'm always transformed by certain books. That's a function of being a book critic. There's a certain level of excitement and revelation that occurred between the writer and the book.

And you say you are constantly being transformed, even by the same books?

Of course. If a book is important to you, you keep on reading it. I reread many books. The Bible, the Old and New Testaments. When I reread certain passages in Plato, a bit of the "Cave" in *The Republic* and that sort of thing, I'm transported. Anything that makes me feel that somebody I'm reading has a great and wonderful mind and a great view of life, transports me.

You mentioned in the opening section of *New York Jew*, which I love, Room 315 at the New York Public Library. You spent five years making your way, reading, to be able to write your first book. You mention that you had an almost ecstatic experience in Room 315, when you had long, full-day bouts with reading.

Yes, yes.

Do you continue to have long bouts like that?

As much as I can for a man of eighty-two. And like any gentleman of eighty-two, I have physical problems. But, of course, as you can tell from my recent book *God and the American Writer*, I still work with the same intensity that I always did. I may be slowing up in a year or two, but at the moment I am okay.

When you were working with that first book, did you expect that you would spend your entire career studying American literature?

No, not at all. I expected nothing except to be drafted. It was during the war period. And when I finished my book, I was indeed summoned by the draft board. It was war time. You know what was going on. I had no expectations. The success of the book surprised me. I was very glad. But I also had personal problems, personal things, which interested me much more at that point.

A question or two back, you mentioned the function of the critic; do you have a sense of your reader? Do you have a sense of whom you are writing for?

Oh, absolutely. A lot of professors write for each other. I do write for what Virginia Woolf called the common reader. I am a common reader myself. I just wrote a piece for the *New York Times Book Review* about the English writer V. S. Pritchett. When I read him, he is talking to me, and I learn from him. When I write something and a writer says to me, "I never thought of that before," that is very, very good. I don't aim at the reader. I aim to express what I myself most deeply feel. But if you do that successfully then the reader receives your message.

Do you hear from your readers?

Of course, of course. A lot of people write to me.

I just came back from San Francisco where the new library there sent 200,000 books off to the landfill because there was no room for them on the new shelves. How do you respond to something like this, and do you think about the fate of books at all?

Of course. Everybody knows what's going on right now. There's no question that television and movies and the media generally have taken away a lot of the appeal of reading. People do not read the way they used to. On the other hand, there's a vast publication industry, but of course, there's a great interest in getting bestsellers. I think that literacy is not what it used to be. I was just reading a book the other night, *When Russia Learned to Read*.

I don't know it.

But there is a very interesting statistic. They were able to look at census figures, people who were able to sign their names and that kind of thing. In 1897, only 21 percent of the Russian population could read. And yet this was coming right out of a period when you had the very great Russian novelists—there's nothing surprising about that. Russia was a closed society, there was no liberty, no freedom. That's why my mother and father, they were born in Russia, eventually found their way individually to America. Also, the great Russian writers, up to Chekhov, were all aristocrats. They belonged to a very special class.

So they were writing for their peers?

No, they weren't writing for their peers. No, no.

Well, then, that's my point: If 80 percent of the people in their country couldn't read, whom were they writing for?

Well, enough people read them, and also they had a vast international audience.

I guess I'm trying to put it in context. People are saying, "Well, literacy is declining in this nation." I wonder if that is relevant to whether or not serious literature will continue to be produced regardless of how many people there will be to read it.

Well, that question is raised all the time, and you will be happy to hear that I have no answer whatever. Everybody knows that every day there is some new young novelist, and there are all sorts of new people coming into the literary world—women, blacks, Hispanics—who never wrote before. I mean, after all, there weren't many Jewish writers at the beginning of the twentieth century, and now, since the Forties, there have been a great many. We've all been liberated, we've all been sprung free to write.

To go back to Russia, there was a vast population in Russia, and that small percentage of literate people nevertheless involved a great many readers, and Tolstoy and all the great Russian writers wrote for a general audience the way Victor Hugo did in France, the way Dickens did in England.

I gather from what I have read that you certainly consider Faulkner the great American novelist of the twentieth century.

Yes, I do.

And Melville the great American novelist of the nineteenth century.

What are you striving for?

It's interesting that they both were basically rejected in their lifetimes, and you also hear that Melville, in a moment of pique, hid *Billy Budd* for the twentieth century.

Now, wait a second, wait a second. You're talking too loosely here. In the first place, Melville was rejected, and he stopped writing, and there is no question about that. He wrote poetry near the end of his life, privately published. I say all that in my book. And he was supported by an uncle, and then he made a living as a customs inspector. Faulkner was not rejected in any way.

Perhaps not rejected in the same sense, but you mention that his books had gone out of print and that it was Malcolm Cowley that...

Excuse me, but the fact remains that Faulkner is an original. Many people, including myself in *On Native Grounds*, didn't pay proper appreciation to him because he is so original. But all his great books, his greatest books, were written in the 1930s and published in the 1930s and '40s. But you can hardly speak of rejection for a man who at one time had to make a living writing motion pictures, but on the other hand got the Nobel Prize, and became the great figure. So there's no real comparison.

Rejection is a very severe word. But by the same token, you mention that it was Malcolm Cowley who was very influential in reviving his career and in bringing an appreciative readership to his work.

Yes, that is true, he was.

Do you think Faulkner would still enjoy the same stature he does today without Cowley's intervention?

Yes. Cowley didn't perform any miracles.

But he did bring out *The Portable Faulkner,* and that gave him a new life.

He did a lot, but the fact remains that Faulkner owes a lot of his reputation to universities, especially in the South, and Faulkner was the hero of a great many Southern writers. And they did a great deal to bring him back.

To go back to Melville, and to separate him off from Faulkner: Is it a phenomenon that somebody so ahead of his time does have to wait awhile for a new generation to accept him?

Now you ask me a question. You are a literary reporter, right?

Yes, sir.

But you know the answer as well as I do to that. You can't think of any examples for yourself?

Of course I can, but I want to hear your views.

The most famous example is Emily Dickinson, who was hardly published at all in her lifetime.

Did she want to be published, in your view?

I think she did, but there was no opportunity, for one reason or another.

She was discouraged, actually.

She was, and she wasn't. The question didn't come up until her death. She wasn't discouraged, and she wasn't encouraged. She was all alone. The idea of a spinster living in the leading family of Amherst and writing poetry didn't mean much to people. People were not as open as they are right now about these things.

You mention how you got to know Robert Frost, you would walk with him one-on-one, you would be an audience of one. I'm wondering how much influence does it have, what effect, what impact does it have on you to go beyond the work and to know the author personally?

If I know the author, as I got to know Frost, by accident, by virtue of my being, briefly, a professor at Amherst College, it means a great deal. But it doesn't mix up your value of the work. I never met Emily Dickinson, but I know what she was like, and I love her poetry. It all depends upon your contact with a writer.

Had you known Faulkner, do you think...

I couldn't have known Faulkner. Faulkner was extremely asocial. A friend of mine once saw him in the waiting room at Random House, waiting to see his editor, and my friend got very excited and went over to him, hoping to have a conversation. Faulkner rebuffed him and said, "I didn't come here to talk." I only saw him once in my life, when he won the National Book Award for one of his inferior novels, the one about the First World War [*A Fable*]. And then he just mumbled a few words to the audience and walked off.

There's a wonderful story about how Bennett Cerf gave a party for Faulkner one night, and Alfred Knopf came with some books that he wanted him to sign, and Faulkner refused to do it. He said, "I make money doing these things."

I don't believe that for a minute.

It's in Joseph Blotner's biography of Faulkner.

I don't believe that. It's in Blotner's biography?

Yes.

I don't think Faulkner said that. But anyway, when a man like Blotner writes a biography, he's like someone picking up every little morsel he can. Is that important, talking about Faulkner?

No, of course not, but you point out that Faulkner chose art over religion. I think that's very important.

Yes it is, indeed. I am very proud of that sentence. Because the point is that the South around him, especially in his own home town of Oxford, was full of that Southern religion, which he didn't have and had no interest in.

I didn't know that Edmund Wilson actually explored the caves where the Dead Sea Scrolls were found. You mention that he traveled...

Wait a minute, wait a minute. I didn't say he explored the caves.

I don't mean explore, literally. I mean...

He went down there. He didn't explore.

I don't mean explore in the literal sense.

Excuse me, but your facts are not right. I never said he explored...

Of course, he didn't explore, but he went there to look at the place, to view it, to absorb the ambiance, get a sense of...

Yes, he did that.

That's what I'm trying to say.

The only people who explored the caves were...

I'm not trying to suggest that he was an archaeologist. I mean that he was there to...

The only people who explored the caves were the original shepherds, whoever they were, who found the stuff in the cave. Mr. Wilson was too fat, and often too drunk, to get on his knees in a cave.

Mr. Kazin, please, I didn't mean explore in the sense of archaeology. I know he didn't discover the Dead Sea Scrolls. It was an unfortunate use of the word; I meant in terms of going to absorb the ambiance.

Well, of course, that's exactly so. Wilson was fascinated by languages. As you already know, he didn't have any personal interest in religion, but he was a fantastic scholar. Everything interested him. He had the greatest aptitude for languages I've ever encountered. I say that in my book. He was reading every language. So when the discovery was made—he called himself a journalist in the best sense of the word—he went down there, to Qumran, and all those places around the Dead Sea, to see what it was like. He describes it in his book, *The Dead Sea Scrolls*. But he didn't do any exploring.

Honestly, sir, believe me, I didn't mean to suggest he was an archaeologist. I meant it in the sense that he went to get something, and I guess what I was trying to lead to is your own travels.

What travels?

Do you try and go places where…

No, no. I no longer do any of that.

But you did. You've done that, of course.

I've done that. In 1967, I was very lucky to be sent by *Harper's* to do something about the Israeli war there. During the Second World War, I was not a soldier, but I was a reporter in England, and that gave me a lot of stuff. But I did that, not out of a journalistic thing, but because I had the permission. When *Native Grounds* came out in 1942, the Rockefeller Foundation was very pleased that I had published a book; they had given me a fellowship to study for it. There was a big program going on in England, an educational program in the Army, which they wanted to document, and since I was free to travel, and I was dying to travel, it was a perfect match. And I went there, and I spent the last six or seven months of the war in England. I wrote about that in several of my books. It was a big experience for me. But otherwise, I never did much journalistic writing. The long essay on Israel, the 1967 war, I did for *Harper's*. But since then I haven't done very much.

How about in this country? Have you traveled?

Yes, I have. I have, but not always. The big events of my life, I describe in my book. They are all in my book. I've concealed nothing.

I'm not an inventive writer, any more than Wilson was. I write about my experiences. In the 1940s, the great photographer Henri Cartier-Bresson and I were assigned to do a piece for *Harper's Bazaar* on lower New York and the bridges and all that, especially the Brooklyn Bridge, which has been a lifelong icon of my life. So we did that, and I wrote an article for *Harper's Bazaar*.

Wilson, for example, was sent abroad by the *New Yorker* during the Second World War to do what he could, whereas I have done a lot of traveling, but it was mostly because of my visiting teaching. I've been a visiting professor in many countries. It's all based on *Native Grounds*. In Europe and elsewhere—and I've lectured in Russia and Japan and Germany and England, etc., etc.,—but in all those cases I was in a foreign country because I was a visiting professor, not because I had been assigned to go there.

I'm talking specifically about this country.

I know, I said that. New York has always been an obsession of mine, but as I say, that piece I did for *Harper's Bazaar* was pretty much it. I've done a lot of travel writing about America, but almost always because I was a visiting lecturer somewhere, or I was a visiting professor somewhere.

I guess you've never felt that you've had to go to a place, like Pittsfield—where Melville lived for thirteen years in western Massachusetts—to look out on Mt. Greylock the way Melville might have and feel what he may have felt about that mountain to have dedicated *Pierre* to it?

As a matter of fact, I did go to western Massachusetts.

That's what I'm asking you.

But that was because of my literary interest in Melville.

That's what I'm trying to get at.

Well, I did go. I did go to Arrowhead, his house, and I did see Mt. Greylock through a window.

And when you're doing something like that, do you try and imagine what might have moved him to dedicate *Pierre*, for instance, to this mountain?

I don't think that way. When I saw Mt. Greylock, I was glad to see it. I'm interested in authors' lives because I'm interested in authors, period, always have been. Sometimes there's a connection with the work, sometimes there's not, but authors themselves are fascinating beings.

Would you, and please don't consider this a trite question, but would you say that you are a product of your reading, of the books that you have read?

No. I'm a product of my ancestry, of the Brooklyn neighborhood where I was born. Reading has been a great part of my life, but I'm not a product of my reading. You can't put it that way. The answer is that I am a product of a lot of things. I am very much a product of Jewish history, of Jewish experience, of my parents' poverty, of this and that.

That correspondence between Melville and Hawthorne, what a tragedy that Melville destroyed the letters he received from Hawthorne. Do you have any sense of why he might have done that?

It is quite clear that Melville was very taken with Hawthorne, admired him very much. A lot of people have tried to make some kind of incipient homosexual thing out of this. I don't think so. Hawthorne was not only a very happily married man but very sexual. And of course you know, if you have read *Billy Budd*, that partly because of his long life as a sailor, Melville was not unacquainted with what goes on aboard a ship. But the most important thing is, it was not a sexual thing that drew him to Hawthorne. It was the recognition that here was a genius like himself, but a genius that was recognized while he was still unrecognized. The letters that Melville wrote to Hawthorne are all available.

And they are all magnificent.

Beyond magnificent. It is quite obvious that Melville admired Hawthorne—*Moby-Dick* was dedicated to Hawthorne. And Hawthorne admired him very much. But they were very different people. Hawthorne was a thoroughly married man. Melville had a very unhappy marriage in many ways, and it was obvious that—now, I am only guessing; I have never seen any of it—it is obvious that Hawthorne's letters could not have been sufficient for the kind of feeling he was seeking.

He was probably disappointed.

Probably.

Perhaps they didn't give the approbation that…

Now, I didn't say that.

I know you didn't say that. I was asking if perhaps that is what you meant?

I think he wanted some kind of recognition and feeling, and I think Hawthorne gave him that, but what he couldn't give him was the intensity. Melville's letters to Hawthorne are the most intense letters ever written to my knowledge by one writer to another. They are extraordinary. They are wonderful. But Hawthorne was a very different kind of personality. He was all closed up. You might say that Hawthorne was always classical and Melville was always romantic. But I give that as a kind of approximation.

You mention that you can't think of another case where one writer's reading of another has, to use your word, transformed…

Excuse me, I didn't say that. There is no end of writers who discover everything from reading another writer. It is not at all unusual.

Well, can you think of any other cases that are as dramatic as this?

Well, I don't know. Are you telling me, or are you asking me?

I am asking you.

There are many such cases. Whitman, for example, was inspired by Emerson. That famous sentence where Melville wrote one genius recognizes another and they come together—it is very common. Writers depend upon each other in a very great sense. American literature is filled with this. Emily Dickinson was inspired by hymns of the seventeenth century. She was very much inspired by Carlyle and Mrs. Browning. In the twentieth century for example, a lot of French writers—think of Camus—were very much influenced by Faulkner. In Paris, in 1945, I was lucky enough to hear Camus talk about Faulkner, whom he called Foolkneer, and he said, "I love Faulkner. I love the dust and the heat in his work. I am a Southerner myself." What is remarkable about the Melville-Hawthorne correspondence is that Melville was so intense and so excited about the whole thing. But the influence is very common.

I heard you speak about ten years ago at a seminar given by the National Book Critics Circle, and you said at that time that the one contemporary author you read with particular pleasure is Robert Stone. I wonder if I could ask you the same question now?

I read Robert Stone. I am very fond of Richard Ford and people like that.

Do you read contemporary American literature that much?

Not as much as I used to. I don't keep up the way I used to.

So your focus still, in your view, is the nineteenth century?

No, it is not. I didn't say that. What I said is that I don't keep up as much as I used to. What I am writing now is a review of a new novel by Russell Banks, a historical novel about John Brown. I read whatever I can, but I do have very strong interest in the past.

Do you feel that fiction has to be relevant? That is a word we see thrown around by a lot of various factions of criticism today in this debate that is going on over the canon, particularly in the

academy. A book must be *relevant* to be read. Do you have any thoughts on that?

I don't understand what you are saying. The word relevance doesn't mean anything. If you are talking about the fact that there is a canon or that there should be a canon and that lot of writers—blacks, women, homosexuals—are trying to enlarge it, that is one thing. Are you saying that there are writers who want American literature to be more relevant to their experience?

That is what they say, not me. But yes, that is what I am asking.

Of course that goes on. This is a thriving country. There are always people coming up and saying, "Hey, look at me. I am writing about the Bronx." Well, take Don DeLillo for instance. He comes from the Bronx, an Italian family. Forty or fifty years ago there wouldn't have been any interest in a book like that. So what is the question?

I guess I was looking for a general comment on this debate that seems to continue on literary canons.

Well, it doesn't interest me very much, because I take it for granted that there is always an infusion of new blood and that there should be. I represent new blood from the point of view of traditional American literature. I am the first native American from my family. My parents didn't speak English. So that was new blood in 1942 for me to write a book called *On Native Grounds*. A lot of this debate goes on in the universities, but that part doesn't interest me at all, because I don't care for academic critics who are interested mostly in exhibiting what they think of as their method. My idea of critics, and I say this in many books, is a writer like V. S. Pritchett or Edmund Wilson, a writer who just writes for the glory of reading literature and has no particular formula.

Pritchett was largely self-educated from his own reading.

Yes, he was. He was in the leather trade. He never went to university. Read my forthcoming piece in the *New York Times Book*

Review. And he said it was his good luck, he wasn't hidebound, he wasn't kept in by anything. A lot of university people take themselves much too seriously.

What I hear and what I was told is that Amherst College graduated an English major, summa cum laude, who had never taken a course in Shakespeare. That concerns me.

It should concern you.

How is it that somebody could proclaim to be an English major and have never studied Shakespeare on the university level?

I have been a professor at many colleges. A lot of colleges are like closed corporations, you know? Amherst College, where I taught unhappily for three years, is a place that always has formulas. Formulas. I was a writer there, and they had an English course where you had to prescribe a kind of semantics, and I said, "I am not interested." So I had my own chair of American literature. But they didn't like me, and I didn't like them because I wasn't interested in that kind of formula. And one of the terrible things about universities is they always have a special idea of limitations. If there is a guy in English who never read Shakespeare, well, someone should be shot, and it's not Shakespeare. But this sort of thing goes on all the time.

It's disconcerting that we're allowing political considerations to shape conceptions of literature.

There is a difference. There is a difference. If you are involved in a country like the United States which is full of great political and racial problems, you can't help writing and touching on these things. Can a black write a novel without touching on the fact that he is black? And that his great-grandfather was a slave? Of course not. It's one thing, however, to write about conditions the way *Uncle Tom's Cabin* did or Ralph Ellison did in his very good book *Invisible Man*. It's something else to say, "You cannot write about this, or you don't have to take Shakespeare." All that is just bunk.

I have to comment on Melville and the Holy Land chapter. I thought that was brilliant.

Thank you. Anything about Melville is of the greatest interest to me. I'm trying to write a short story that is based upon Melville as an old man in New York. It's called "Sailor Home From the Sea." I haven't written it yet, I'm just thinking about it. But I would take liberties with the actual facts that present him. He was forgotten when he died, you know.

Totally.

Well, they have more than made up for that, haven't they?

And then *Billy Budd* is discovered, what, in 1922?

It was discovered by a graduate student, Raymond Weaver, who went to Melville's granddaughter, Eleanor Metcalf, and they found the book in a red container. But Melville didn't want it published, perhaps. It's a wonderful book. It's a work of genius, that book, but he had sort of given up.

Thankfully he didn't destroy it as he destroyed the letters he had received from Hawthorne.

That's a different thing. He didn't destroy his own work.

So he had faith, you think, in his work.

No, no. You have got to understand the creative process. A man like Melville, who was a failure in the public market, who was getting old, was haunted by the stories of the sea, which was the big thing in his life. So he's haunted also by the erotic relationship story between Claggart and between Billy Budd. He's writing about good and evil, because Billy Budd is so innocent, and he doesn't know what's happening to him. So he writes it.

Your first question to me was, "Am I thinking about my career?" Perhaps some big bestseller writer like Stephen King thinks about his career and the money. But he's not a writer. He manufactures books and that sort of thing. But Melville was not thinking about his career. He had no career, and Faulkner was not thinking about his career when he wrote a book called *The Sound and the Fury*, which was turned down by publisher after publisher. Writers don't think that way. Only businessmen do.

Louis L'Amour

*Interviewed in Boston on July 21, 1982,
to discuss the author's body of work.*

It's anybody's guess how many million readers Louis Dearborn L'Amour already has gobbling up his frontier novels as soon as they reach the stands, but a few facts may help sharpen the focus. At last count, L'Amour had written eighty-five novels, and three new titles appear each year. His publisher, Bantam Books, reports that current figures show there are 125 million copies of his books in print worldwide, translated into nineteen languages as diverse as Japanese, Greek, Norwegian, and Serbo-Croatian.

Of these, thirty-five have been produced into movies, the most popular being *Hondo*, *Shalako*, *Heller in Pink Tights*, *The Burning Hills*, and *Catlow*. Additionally, he has written scripts for sixty-five television shows, most notably for Walt Disney Productions.

L'Amour is undoubtedly one of America's best-selling living novelists. His work is celebrated even in the hallowed halls of Congress. Earlier this month, the U.S. House of Representatives voted to strike a gold medal for L'Amour, along with the former heavyweight champion Joe Louis and the musician Fred Waring. And yet, for all this, there remains one small problem.

If you're a fan of the Western, then you know the man and his work. The *New York Times* reported a few years ago that L'Amour's books are more popular among America's truck drivers than girlie magazines and road maps. His following is solidly devoted and surprisingly diverse. But when's the last time you saw L'Amour's name on a bestseller list? When's the last time, for that matter, that you saw one of his books reviewed in a major newspaper, magazine, or periodical?

Answer to both: hardly ever.

One reason may be that the vast majority of L'Amour's books have never been published in hardbound, and only hardbound books are tallied on the major lists. Original paperbacks are rarely reviewed, and critics, moreover, tend to ignore Westerns as they do other works that fall into specific genres, like science fiction, mystery, and romance.

For L'Amour, who recently rode into Boston on a reader-reconnaissance mission, this kind of treatment is not only unfair, it's hypocritical. "If a man is in bed with another man's wife, that's considered literature," he said with straightforward simplicity. "If the subject is the opening up of half the country, that's not, and it's absurd."

But don't think for a moment that this neglect by the literati bothers him all that much. "Bantam sold seven million of my books last year alone," he added. "What I do is write for readers, and millions of people out there are reading my books. They seem happy with what I'm doing, and that's what counts. If the critics review them, fine. If they don't, that's fine, too. It doesn't disturb me in the least."

There are any number of reasons why L'Amour is the best-read writer in the history of the Western—better even than Zane Grey or Max Brand—but the one most cited by aficionados is his obsession for authenticity and accuracy. That, of course, and a natural talent for spinning a good yarn.

A tenth-generation American born in Jamestown, North Dakota (he won't say how long ago), L'Amour now lives with his wife of twenty-six years and two teen-aged children in a Spanish-style villa in Beverly Hills. His study boasts two electric typewriters, each one assigned to a different novel. When L'Amour tires of working on one, he swivels around in his chair and picks up the thread of the other.

"Sometimes I switch at lunchtime," he said. "Sometimes I may go several days without working on one of them, then I'll come back to it. But I work every single day, seven days a week. I love to write. I'd rather do that than anything else in the world."

How long it takes him to write a novel, though, he wouldn't say. "There's no way to answer how long it takes to write a book. Sometimes I'm thinking about them for months and years. I write three books a year; that should cover it pretty well."

As for rewriting, "I do no revisions at all," he answered matter-of-factly. "One time through the typewriter, and then I correct the typos. That's it. But I do a lot of thinking beforehand. When I start, I never have my ending in sight. I have the general trend of my story and where it will take place. What I do is begin with a situation and a couple of characters and take it from there."

Helping L'Amour achieve the authenticity that distinguishes his novels is a private library numbering more than 10,000 volumes. On his recent trip through Canada and New England, L'Amour bought another hundred books for his collection. He rarely reads other novelists, focusing instead on research material.

"Contrary to what a lot of people think, we don't have to guess what happened on the frontier. We know because there were people there at the time writing it all down," L'Amour noted. "I cover the field. I study diaries and journals, all kinds of small-town newspapers. Lots of times readers send me interesting things in the mail. Stories come out of the woodwork every time you turn around."

One of the great myths he likes to explode is the romantic status the gunfighter enjoys in Western lore. "The gunfighter was common, but he didn't occupy any position of honor. Some of them did, but they were honored for other reasons. Gunfights, for the most part, took place on the wrong side of the tracks, in the red-light districts, out on the range, places like that. Most of the people went to church on Sundays, sent their kids to school, and worked, just like we do."

But what identified the everyday person of the period, he added, was toughness. "They weren't intimidated by anyone. Now you take Jesse James and the Cole Younger gang, a pretty mean bunch of fellows. They decided to rob two banks out in Northfield, Minnesota, which wasn't even a real Western town, as towns went. Well, they went in there and got shot to pieces by a bunch of farmers and businessmen. You have to realize that all of these people grew up using guns. If you didn't shoot meat for the table, you didn't eat. And most of the adult men were veterans of the Civil War, so you were dealing with a pretty hardy group of people."

L'Amour is noted also for his knowledge of Indians—their many tribes, habits, customs, and frequently stormy encounters with the white man. "Some people may know more than me about some individual tribes," he said, "but I don't think there are many people who know more about all of them. And I'm still learning all the time, believe me."

His view on the conquest of the continent from Native Americans might, however, surprise a few people. "We Americans are masochistic in that respect. We like to punish ourselves; we like to beat ourselves with a stick. We did nothing here that wasn't done all over the world and hasn't been done since the beginning of time. After all, in England there were the Picts, who were moved out by the Celts, who were moved out by the Saxons, who were moved out by the Normans. Each one took over from the other one, and nobody cried about it."

There were Indians, he added, who took land from other Indians. "There were good and bad people on both sides, a two-way street. There were a lot of noble savages, as the saying goes, but they were only noble at certain times, and the same thing with the white man. There was a vast difference between tribes. I write about Indians with sympathy, but I tell the truth. They were here, and they had the land. They despised the white man from the beginning. The first whites who came wanted to buy furs. To an Indian, if he was any kind of man, why didn't he trap his own furs? What are you, a woman? Gradually, though, the Indian wanted a lot of things that he could only get from the white man, and he dealt with him."

To study L'Amour's intimidating list of credits might give the impression that he has been writing all his life, but he is a man who has spent a lot of time away from the typewriter following an astonishing variety of pursuits. Morley Safer suggested several years ago in a *60 Minutes* feature that L'Amour was sixty-eight years old, but that was just a guess, and L'Amour offered nothing to set the record straight.

"I don't tell anyone my age for philosophic reasons," he said. "I was in World War II, so that should give you some idea. I just don't believe anyone should tell their age because it's a way to judge people. If you judged Winston Churchill on the first fifty years of his life, you'd have nobody worth talking about."

However old L'Amour is, he is undeniably sturdy and fit. He has a full head of salt-and-pepper hair, his handshake is firm and sure, Western-style clothes complement his husky frame perfectly. The string tie around his neck set off an attractive Indian design in silver and turquoise; the only other item of jewelry apparent was a solid gold bracelet with "LOUIS" boldly engraved on its face.

"I left home in North Dakota when I was fifteen years old," he said. "I weighed 155 pounds and I passed for twenty-two. Then I passed for twenty-four until I was twenty-four. The jobs I got were the jobs that were available at the time. Those first few years were very rough. I was on the move. It was bad times, and I missed a lot of meals. I was hungry a lot. The first job I got was in Texas skinning dead cattle out in the Panhandle. These were cattle that had been dead for a while. Their meat wasn't any good, but you could still skin them for their hides."

At other times, he worked as a lumberjack, longshoreman, elephant handler, hay shocker, flume builder, fruit picker, and merchant seaman who "knocked around a good deal" in the Orient, West Indies, and Europe. Every episode has a tale, and every tale inspired the telling of others.

"I used to fight a little bit," he said parenthetically, explaining why his earliest short articles (some 800 in all, over the years) were about boxing. "I had fifty-nine fights. I lost five. I started out as a middleweight and fought most of my fights as a light heavyweight." He fought under a variety of names, he added, but he doesn't disclose any of them. "I won't say because, in the first place, none of them were very well known. Nobody knew who the hell I was. I fought all over the states and some abroad. My toughest and longest fight was fought over in Borneo."

Was he any good at it?

"Yes," he said after a pause, "if you don't mind my saying so, I was. I knocked out thirty-four guys, and the only fights I lost was when I wasn't eating regularly." What it takes to be a good fighter, he added, is what it takes to be a prolific writer. "In the first place, you've got to be hungry. You've got to want to win very badly, and I was hungry and I wanted to win. The major lesson I learned from fighting is to get up after you've been knocked down and keep on slugging until you win. As a writer, you get a lot of rejection slips, but if you keep getting up, eventually you'll win."

Though in those days, L'Amour harbored some idle thoughts about making a career of boxing, "I always knew I was going to write. I wanted to tell stories before I was big enough to walk. My great-grandfather was killed and scalped by Indians. I grew up on Indian stories and stories of the frontier. I had a brother who rode down on the Mexican border in 1916, during the Pancho Villa days. I acquired an awful lot of background that I didn't really intend to use. Actually, I intended to write about other things, not about the West, because it was too close to home."

Consequently, his first stories dealt with boxing, seafaring, the Far East—places that had charged his imagination. "I knew right from the start that I was going to make it. My mother once asked me after repeated failures what I was going to do if I didn't make it. I told her that idea never entered my mind."

It wasn't until after the war that "I really got going," he said. His first novel, *Westward the Tide*, was published in England in 1950. The event that changed his life dramatically came two years later, though, when a paperback editor read one of his short stories—"The Gift of Cochise"—in *Collier's* magazine. "He called me and said he'd be interested in a novel based on that story. I did it, and everybody wanted stories on the frontier from me after that."

Most of L'Amour's novels stand by themselves, but a few years back he introduced three families—the Sacketts, the Chantrys, and the Talons—who appear in a number of his novels. The idea there, he explains, is to recreate the story of the birth and expansion of the American frontier, territory by territory, over three centuries through the lives of these families. He projects at least forty volumes in this saga alone.

"I got the idea for the families partly through my wife," he pointed out. "In going through a record of her family history, it occurred to me that her people and my people must have crossed paths many times over the course of the past two hundred years. If it's true of us, it must be true of a lot of people. So I got the idea of telling the story of the opening of the American frontier through their eyes."

When he writes, he writes "as if a man of the period was going to be looking at this. He's always in the back of my mind, and I keep thinking, if he were about to read this story, what would he think about it? If I'm pleasing him, then I'm pleasing today's readers. They have come to realize I'm writing a story that's based on truth."

L'Amour is entirely self-taught in subjects as wide ranging as geology, ecology, geography, and cartography. "An editor once omitted one of my footnotes," he recalled. "It explained that a certain type of gun—a scraper—was only made as a test model. I got thousands of letters from frontier buffs and gun people."

But in addition to his documentary research, L'Amour has known many people, including some thirty old gunfighters, who have helped pump blood into his characters. These men have become romantic figures around the world, he said, for many reasons.

"I think a lot of it has to do with the man on horseback; he's always been a romantic figure. The West was a romantic period, though just what romance is is hard to define. It was a time when a lot of things were happening, a lot of what we call adventure. Adventure is just a romantic name for trouble. That's all it is."

Most of the interesting frontiersmen, he said, were, above all else, individuals. "He didn't work well on a team. He wasn't a loner in the common sense, but he was on his own. When he got fed up, he just got on his horse and rode off into the sunset or whatever, and left everything behind."

For all the appeal and romance of the Old West, though, L'Amour is happy to be living now and not then. "I'd rather live now than any other time in the world's history. Everything else that's happened in the world is just preliminary to what's happening now, because now, we're going to take off into space. The greatest frontier of all is ahead of us—the frontier that's endless."

He is pleased that he has millions of readers, but he figures roughly there are twenty-five million more people he should be able to reach. Yet, the question arises, why isn't he satisfied with an already enviable constituency? "I want them all," he said with the zeal of an evangelist, adding with the salt of a sailor, "I want every damned one of them."

Yes, but again, why?

"I want to set the record straight," he said with soft-spoken conviction. "I want people to learn about their country. I want to pass the history on."

Occasionally, he said, he goes back and reads some of his earlier novels. "I didn't for a long time, but every once in a while somebody will ask me some question that I've forgotten, so I have to go back and read them."

Is he ever concerned that sometimes, perhaps, he might repeat himself in a book?

"Never," he said emphatically. "That isn't possible because there are so many areas I haven't even touched on yet."

Finally, after so much success and so many fans solidly in his camp, is Louis L'Amour still hungry?

"Only for more time," he answered philosophically. "I still got a lot of books I want to write, and I haven't even begun to scratch the surface, to tell you the truth."

Lynda La Plante

Interviewed in Boston on April 17, 1996, for Cold Shoulder.

Whenever she needs material to use in one of her hard-boiled thrillers or award-winning TV scripts, the writer Lynda La Plante has learned there is no substitute for reality. "I have to get the genuine goods," the author of *Bella Mafia* and *Entwined* said last week in a Boston interview. And to get it, La Plante is willing to pay various "experts" serious money for their knowledge. This commitment to authenticity has brought her two Emmys and an Edgar Allan Poe award for the PBS TV series *Prime Suspect*, and a growing reputation as the author of no-holds-barred novels.

Cold Shoulder, her latest book, offers yet another case in point. Lorraine Page, the principal character, is a former Los Angeles homicide detective whose descent into alcoholism and prostitution occasions contact with a serial killer who preys on down-and-out women like herself. Driven by untapped reservoirs of grit and inner strength, she reclaims her dignity, pursues the killer, restores her self-esteem, and begins a new life.

"What makes the premise particularly compelling," La Plante said, "is that it is absolutely true. This character is modeled on one tough, very hard, and not very likable woman. But that's okay with me because I, for one, don't think it terribly necessary that we like the people we're reading. What matters is that they are credible human beings."

The idea for the Lorraine Page character—whose appearance here is the debut performance in what is intended as a continuing series—came as the result of extensive press coverage in Los Angeles for La Plante's work on the *Prime Suspect* TV series.

"I had told several interviewers out there that if someone comes to me with a good story idea, I am prepared to buy it. I have done it frequently in the past; I will do it now," La Plante said. "Barely a day went by when this woman came to see me at the Bel Air Hotel, where nobody knew I was staying, and announced she has a story she wants to sell me. I told her to explain to me in a few sentences why I should be interested in her story. She did this, and I told her that is a very good story indeed. She said, 'Fine, my lawyer is outside in the car.' He came in, and we did the deal on the spot."

The woman told La Plante how she was forced to leave the police department eight years earlier after mistakenly shooting a fourteen-year-old boy during a nighttime chase, and how the subsequent loss of her husband and children led to a degraded life on skid row. "I sold my body, I sold everything I had, and eight years later I'm clean, I'm back, and I'm a private detective," the woman said.

In return for money, she not only outlined the events of her life, she also showed La Plante her former haunts and furnished precise details of various crimes that had been committed. She also demanded that her true identity be concealed. "By paying for information, you never feel that you're intruding," La Plante said. "I can keep going back for more, because we have a deal."

A native of England, La Plante trained as an actress at the Royal Academy of the Dramatic Arts, acted in London with the Royal Shakespeare Company and the National Theatre, and performed soap opera parts on British television. She now divides her time between London and East Hampton, Long Island.

During the early Eighties, La Plante had an idea for a British TV drama called *Widows* that was based on real people. "It was the first time they'd ever had a series in England that starred five women without a male lead, and it was a monster hit." Each of the women was the widow of a bank robber who had died in a bomb blast while preparing for a big heist. The women get together, train, and pick up where the men left off.

"What made it seem so real was the authenticity I wrote into it," La Plante said. "I got to know the wives of some robbers, I spent time with them, met their husbands, interviewed a few of them in prison."

The success of the six-hour miniseries in England prompted a huge sale to Disney Studios and La Plante's first trip to Hollywood. "When I got there, I discovered this extraordinary thing," she recalled. "They had outbid every single studio and bought this script, but nobody had read it, nobody had even looked at the video. So they asked me to 'pitch' it at a meeting. I did this, and they looked at me and said, 'Where are the laughs?' I said, 'What do you mean laughs? This is a drama.' They thought they had bought a comedy for Bette Midler. I was right out the door, back on the next plane to England. But I liked the movie business and knew I would be back."

But the key to her own success as a writer, she maintained, is her passion for research and getting it right. "I've discovered over and over and over that fact is a lot better than fiction, and that the clues are always right there in your face," she said. "They're there, looking you in the eyes."

Doris Lessing

Interviewed in New York City on October 24, 1994, for Under My Skin; *Lessing received a Nobel Prize for literature in 2007.*

There is a precision to Doris Lessing, a measured, considered demeanor that is every bit as evident in her conversation as it is in her writing. With more than thirty books to her credit over the past forty-five years—an impressive body of work that includes novels, short stories, poetry, dramas for the stage, and essays published in numerous languages throughout the world—Lessing, seventy-five, has decided to set the record straight about her life in a series of memoirs.

The first of these, *Under My Skin*, has just been published, providing the occasion for an interview in New York City during a visit from her home in London. Because Lessing has been unequivocal over the years about her preference for fiction, and because she has used so much of her own life to inform her writing, the most pressing question, it seemed, was why she now sees the need for an autobiography.

"I learned that there are five people writing books about my life," she said. "I know that they are going to get it all wrong. One of the earliest memories I have is saying to myself, 'Now, this is what happened. Remember it. Don't let them talk you out of it.' So I have these very, very precise moments, and here they are."

Lessing's principal concern is how biographers will deal with her personal life. Most vexing is the matter of having left the two children from her first marriage in Africa with her former husband when she moved to England in 1949, at age thirty, and how her twenty years as a communist will be treated.

"I am writing this book now, at the age of seventy-five and looking back from this perspective," she said. "It would be a different book if I wrote it at eighty-five. It would be a different book if I had written it at the age of fifty.

"Memory can be very creative, but it can also be very slippery. What is important is that I rely in this book only on memories I can vouch for and that I know are true." This first volume concludes the year Lessing left for England, taking with her the manuscript for *The Grass Is Singing*, a powerful novel of a white woman's obsession with her black servant.

The separation from her earlier life was decisive, one that cut her off "from the tentacles of family," she writes. "I was not going home to my family—I was fleeing from it. The door had shut and that was that."

The second volume of memoirs will deal with the 1950s, years that saw Lessing lose all confidence in and respect for the utopian promises of communism, years when she began to write some of her most influential books, including *Martha Quest* (1952), the first of five novels in a series collectively called the Children of Violence, and which drew on her own childhood experiences in British-ruled Rhodesia.

Toward the end of the decade, she began writing *The Golden Notebook*, an experimental work published in 1962 that examines on several levels, and with a minute particularity, the experience of a woman writer. It is considered a landmark book of feminist politics, one that prompted the American novelist Lisa Alther to write that "almost every woman writer I know acknowledges a debt" to Doris Lessing.

Because Lessing commands such unquestioned stature, the frustration she often expresses with modern feminism is difficult to dismiss. "I am very out of sympathy with them," she said flatly. "Like many women of my generation, I'm terribly disappointed because the 1960s explosion of feminism had so much energy behind it, and it's all been frittered away in talk, as far as I'm concerned."

What has happened, she continued, "is that a number of white, middle-class women in America and Europe have very much bettered their own condition, but they haven't touched working-class women or women of the Third World, and I think it was a very much badly structured movement," she said.

"Feminism was not invented in the 1960s," she pointed out. "Women of my generation spent a lot of time wondering how to improve things, and to see this enormous energy just going to waste in squabbles complaining about men, or this ridiculous rubbish about taking men to court for paying them a compliment, is very embarrassing and such a waste."

Lessing is celebrated for her willingness to try different writing forms, including five books in the Canopus in Argos: Archives series, set in another universe. Ten years ago, she also wrote two novels under the name of Jane Somers, hoping to be "published and reviewed on merit." After a number of rejections, one alert British editor said that the first Somers book, *The Diary of a Good Neighbour*, suggested the work "of the young Doris Lessing," and made an offer.

In the United States, the former editor at Alfred A. Knopf, Robert Gottlieb, "recognized it immediately and bought it. But none of the 'Doris Lessing experts' he sent it to caught it in their reviews."

Even though her work is read by millions of people (her story "Through the Tunnel" is widely anthologized for young adults), Lessing insisted that she never writes to entertain. "You're going to the roots of everything when you ask that question," she said. "I think writers like me are always trying to find out something, whatever it is. When I write a book, it's a discovery process, because when I start, yes, I have a story, I have roughly the characters, and I have the tone of voice, which is the most important thing of all. But I know ideas are going to come that I haven't got at the moment, that are going to be new ideas, new insights. And that's very exciting."

It is partly for this reason that she finds writing fiction the most rewarding creative exercise. "The most interesting question, I think, is why is it that a piece of writing that has not one fact in it can be more true than something which is factual, because the atmosphere is right, or the flavor is right?"

In the end, Lessing said, "I'm always writing about experience. When you're doing that, you're writing from your solar plexus, not the top of your head. When you are writing a novel properly, you are writing with all of yourself. You are writing with memories."

Joyce Maynard

*Interviewed in Boston on September 14, 1998,
for* At Home in the World.

The question for memoirist Joyce Maynard is not whether there is sufficient drama in her life to justify the writing of a full autobiography, but whether learning details about the time she spent with the reclusive author J. D. Salinger a quarter-century ago is the only reason some people might have for reading it.

"Did you go straight through from the beginning, or did you jump ahead to the juicy parts?" the forty-four-year-old author of *At Home in the World* asked with a hint of sarcasm at the start of a recent interview in Boston. The answer she received on this occasion—that the Salinger material was read ahead of the purely autobiographical section that appears at the front of the book—elicited another heated observation from a writer who has clearly lost whatever respect she might have had for "the opinion givers" in the media.

"You know, I've been pretty well-behaved on this tour, but I'm getting just a little angry, to tell you the truth, with people who basically want this to be another story, who wish that the story was that when somebody finally got to be with J. D. Salinger, he would be this wise, stately, more-secure-than-all-the-rest-of-us person," she said.

"They are disappointed not just that I am telling the story, but that the story isn't the one they wanted to hear." What is disturbing her most of all, she continued, is that some reviewers are ignoring what she has to say about her own life apart from Salinger. "If you've read this book, you certainly know that it's a book about my whole life."

Still, Maynard readily concedes that the extensive press attention accorded her book, and the sales it consequently has generated, have been shaped measurably by her willingness, after twenty-five years, to discuss the nine months she lived with Salinger, and less by the parallel account she offers of her "whole life."

"I think that J. D. Salinger is definitely worthy of people's attention," she agreed. "But I also believe this story would be just as valid if it were about an eighteen-year-old who spent time with any strong, powerful man."

The focus on the relationship has been "intensified," Maynard believes, because she has finally detailed her experiences with "a person about whom I was forbidden to speak," although she quickly acknowledged that Salinger never specifically told her to remain silent about their time together. "He simply laid down the rules thirty, forty years ago about how he was to be treated, and to an astonishing degree, the world has responded."

Maynard directs particular anger toward Jonathan Yardley, the Pulitzer Prize–winning critic for the *Washington Post* who in August suggested that if *At Home in the World* turned out to be "15 percent as bad" as the lengthy excerpt published that month in *Vanity Fair* magazine, "it will bid fair to be the worst book ever written: smarmy, whiny, smirky and, above all, almost indescribably stupid."

Maynard asserted that what bothers her most about that kind of "blanket condemnation" is that it appeared in print before the book had even been published. "If my definition of success was to get a pat on the back from Jonathan Yardley, I'd be feeling bad right now. But I'm not. I'm proud of the work I've done."

Maynard's pride extends to the publication of five other books, numerous magazine articles, and many newspaper columns she has written over the years that deal variously with her marriage, the birth and raising of her three children, a contentious divorce, an abortion, and her decision to have cosmetic surgery, among other decidedly domestic concerns. One of her books, the novel *To Die For*, was made into a movie starring Nicole Kidman. A good deal of the criticism directed toward *At Home in the World* is that it offers nothing about Salinger as a writer or as a thinker, gives no insight into what has made him the most celebrated literary recluse in the world, and concentrates instead on such mundane matters as his eccentric eating habits and his fondness for vacuous television sitcoms.

"I did not go to his house as a literary critic. I wasn't some *New Yorker* person come to talk about Tolstoy with him," she said. "That just isn't my story. And I have to tell you, I don't think he would have contacted me in the first place if that's who I was."

Maynard by no means was "some *New Yorker* writer" who, in 1972, at the age of eighteen, moved in with a man thirty-five years her senior, but it was the appearance of a spunky article she wrote for the *New York Times Magazine* that prompted the mysterious creator of Holden Caulfield, one of the most influential characters in twentieth-century American fiction, to write her the fan letter that led to their relationship.

Titled "An Eighteen-Year-Old Looks Back on Life," the *Times* article featured Maynard's fetching photograph on the cover of the magazine; she was an eighteen-year-old Yale freshman at the time, to be sure, but she could just as easily have passed for an adolescent of thirteen. Impressed, apparently, with Maynard's glib way of expressing her alienation and weariness with life at such a tender age, Salinger wrote her from his rural home in Cornish, New Hampshire.

"It would have been impossible for me not to answer that letter," Maynard said, even though she admits that prior to hearing from Salinger, she had never read *The Catcher in the Rye*, or anything else he had written for that matter. "For somebody so important and so powerful to tell you, 'You and I are soul-mates,' that goes further than a dozen roses or a diamond necklace."

A fervid correspondence ensued—Maynard has a spate of letters she is unable to quote from directly in the book because of "Jerry" Salinger's well-documented willingness to sue anyone so inclined—with Maynard finally deciding to leave a summer job she had with the *New York Times*, drop out of Yale, and move in with a man she came to regard as "the closest thing I ever had to a religion."

Maynard writes that she was a virgin who had "never seen a naked man" before, yet the relationship would remain unconsummated for various physical reasons, even though what may or may not constitute sex sounds numbingly familiar in light of recent news events. The arrangement ended abruptly when Salinger sent her away in March of 1973.

The attitude of Maynard's parents regarding their daughter's decision to become Salinger's housemate was surprisingly acquiescent, and not one that she is willing to explore at any great depth.

The reader learns how Max Maynard, her father, was an alcoholic college lecturer who was unfairly denied promotions, and how his wife Fredelle gave up a promising academic career to raise a family. What many critics have found lacking, however, is the kind of perceptive examination that might explain their role in shaping their daughter's personality, and the fateful turn she took in her life.

"I had been raised to please, and I was looking for something larger than myself, something outside of me, to attach myself to, to make me feel worthy," Maynard said vaguely about her upbringing, and why she chose to go off and live with Salinger.

"I adored my parents, and I am able to tell their story because, ultimately, I love them, even though I think that what happened was very unwise," she said. "But I stay away from the word 'dysfunctional' when it comes to my family. What I have written is a book about forgiveness, actually. It recognizes that people you love, people that did not set out to hurt you, are to be understood and forgiven."

For all the hostile publicity she has received in the press, Maynard said the readers she has cultivated over the years "are interested in the full story of a woman," and remain her loyal fans now. She noted that since publication of *At Home in the World* last month, her website "is recording forty thousand hits a day," with more than two million people having visited since she launched it last year.

"The response is overwhelmingly supportive," she said. "And these are the people that matter to me."

Arthur Miller

*Interviewed in Boston on December 3, 1987,
for* Timebends, *an autobiography. Miller won a
Pulitzer Prize for his play* Death of a Salesman.

There came a point early on, when success finally arrived after many failed attempts, that the young playwright realized there would be several Arthur Millers. The year was 1947, and after a fitful start that included indifferent reviews from some confused critics, the play *All My Sons* finally achieved commercial success on Broadway, and with that followed increasing respect for the writer's literary skill.

As weeks went on—and as the Coronet Theatre continued to fill its seats with paying customers—Miller realized that his "words had a power beyond my mere self," and he felt "a certain threat along with the inevitable exhilaration," he recalls in *Timebends*, an exceptionally rich autobiography published by Grove Press.

With *All My Sons*, Miller became a celebrity, and soon he found himself greeted on the street by people, "with a glazed expression that made me feel unnervingly artificial. My identification with life's failures was being menaced by my fame." He found himself experiencing "the guilt of success," a feeling reinforced by the "leftist egalitarian convictions" he had nurtured as a youngster growing up in New York and as an undergraduate during the Thirties at the University of Michigan. He expressed this "guilt" thematically and through the characters created in his written work.

"It occurred to me three or four times a day that if I did no work, I would still be earning a lot of money and by the end of the week would be richer than at the beginning," he remembers thinking at the time. But instead of sitting around and collecting his royalties, Miller found that this achievement—his first produced play after ten earlier attempts had ended in failure—liberated him in an exciting kind of way.

"I had won a new freedom to create, and I would stand on the high point of the bridge's arch facing the wind from the ocean, trying to embrace a world larger than I had been able to conceive of until this time. If I had no subject, I had an indescribable feeling of a new form; it would be both infinitely compressed and expansive and leisurely, the story both strange and homely. It would be something never seen on any stage before."

From this resolution emerged two years later a play universally known and admired as *Death of a Salesman*, a play that demonstrated how worship of success can lead to delusion and self-destruction, a play that challenged the basic underpinnings of the American Dream. It is generally regarded as one of the great dramas ever written by an American and certainly one of the most enduring.

The extraordinary success his plays have achieved, his refusal to cooperate with the House Un-American Activities Committee in the Fifties, and his highly publicized marriage to Marilyn Monroe have made him a formidable public figure over the past four decades. Yet, despite all this—probably, in large part, as a result of all this—he has remained an intensely private man. Because he has often been treated ambivalently by critics, he is wary of the press, and openly resents the power New York critics exercise on the fortunes of a play.

He has been interviewed dozens of times over the years, and by all accounts he is unfailingly forthcoming and helpful when the subject is his work and his causes. When the discussion turns to his personal life, though, he is understandably guarded and occasionally abrupt. Such was the case when I interviewed him during a recent visit to Boston.

In *Timebends* there is an especially moving section where Miller describes his initial meeting with Marilyn Monroe in California, and his first parting with her at the Los Angeles airport when he had to go back East to work on a play: "She was in a beige skirt and a white satin blouse and her hair hung down to her shoulders, parted on the right side, and the sight of her was something like pain, and I knew that I must flee or walk into a doom beyond all knowing." Later, when they had started to date, Miller once said to her, "I keep trying to teach myself how to lose you, but I can't learn yet." Her answer: "Why must you lose me?"

Their five-year marriage, which ended in divorce in 1961, had brought together two people seemingly larger than life, one an adored sex goddess, the other a controversial and often radical intellectual. Since he had a sense of foreboding about pursing a relationship with Marilyn Monroe—but continued anyway "into a doom beyond all knowing"—I asked Miller whether he ever considered the two of them anything like characters in a play who must proceed toward an inevitable resolution.

"No human being feels he's a character in a play," Miller replied. "No human being I ever heard of. He's just living his life." He found the suggestion that he often has been perceived as an "autobiographical" playwright equally dismissible. "Those are tags that lazy journalists use, if you'll forgive me," he said.

Then he was reminded that the observation wasn't being made that he chronicled his life in his plays, but that he drew generously from his own experiences for inspiration and based many characters on people he has met or has known. "I'll tell you, the problem is, you see, that most people can't imagine creating anything. So they think that a writer is a reporter. That's the problem. They go looking for the model as though the work were nothing but some kind of a report made of an event. Which is perfectly okay. There have been great books written about actual events. Dostoevsky used to write out of newspaper clippings. There's nothing wrong with that. It's just that it doesn't happen with me."

And a question about why he has been so keenly interested in examining various aspects of the father-son relationship brought this response: "Yes, the father-son thing is central to my work, but it doesn't exist in about half the plays I have written. It's not in *The Crucible*; it's not in *View from the Bridge*; it's not in *Incident at Vichy*. It happens to be the main theme in *Death of a Salesman* and *All My Sons*, those two plays, but thereafter I left it behind and I haven't touched it for forty years."

As the questions moved more toward Miller's attitudes about writing, the more expansive his answers became. He thought a comparison between the structure of several of his plays and *Timebends* quite appropriate, for instance. The memoir follows an unusual narrative form which is often chronological, but which leaps forward and backward when certain experiences trigger related thoughts. *After the Fall* works similarly, and so, too, does *Death of a Salesman*, which frequently fuses the past with the present.

"I don't think time has any place in recollection," he explained. "We don't recall things in relation to time. We recall them by virtue of their relation between one image or another. You recall because one thing obviously suggests another, rather than having anything to do with time. So time is squeezed out of the book in that sense. For me the best form has always been one that leads you most directly to what interests you most." What really matters, he continued, is relationships, a guiding principle he has tried to follow throughout his work. "In a sense, I've always been bending time."

The success of his first produced play, *All My Sons*, was the vehicle that gave him the freedom to experiment with form and resulted in the creation of *Death of a Salesman*. Miller's description of that period in his memoir is one of the most satisfying segments in the book because it offers an uncommonly perceptive view of how the creative process works.

Just what, I asked, is there about the life of Willy Loman that continues to move audiences so profoundly and continues to speak so eloquently about the human condition. "I think it may just be that it's a certain total embrace of a situation, of a man, that you rarely find in anything else," Miller said.

"It's Willy as a private person, as a father, as a lover, as a husband, as a man in his society and in his business, as a son himself, as a brother. Practically every side of his existence is in that play and dramatized in the play. I don't think anybody else has ever tried to make an absolutely total onslaught on to one person like that before. Maybe that's the reason it's always been so popular with audiences."

The suggestion, though, that *Death of a Salesman* is the work that identifies Miller as a playwright more than anything else is not greeted with enthusiasm. "I have never been blocked," Miller said. "And the most produced play I've ever written I wrote right after *Death of a Salesman*, which is *The Crucible*, which has been produced twice as often as *Salesman*, as a matter of fact. Abroad, it's my most famous play, and some people think *A View From the Bridge* is my best play."

Now seventy-two, Miller said he still works every day at his home in Connecticut and that he never worries about whether his best work might be behind him. "I think *Timebends* is among my best work," he said. "I've just written a film which is called *Almost Everybody Wins*, and it will be going into production this spring, and I'm working on a play now. I'm at my desk seven days a week, usually, and I've never been lost for ideas."

While he is best known as a playwright, Miller has demonstrated facility with other literary forms. He has written eloquent essays on the theater; his first book, *Situation Normal*, was assorted journalism;

The Misfits and *Playing for Time* were screenplays; *I Don't Need You Anymore* is a collection of stories; and *Focus*, a novel, was published soon after *All My Sons* was produced. He also has written a book for children and collaborated with his wife, the noted photographer Inge Morath, on several travel books.

Yet, it is the theater—writing for a live audience—that energizes him most, even though American theater finds itself in a most discouraging state of health today. "I might not have been a man of the theater if the theater had been in the condition it is today," he agreed. "It's been betrayed in so many ways now that it barely breathes air. And when I came in I thought it was bad enough, but I never dreamed it would get to this. So if I am a man of the theater it is because there was a theater of some kind then. There was a profession of the theater, and one felt it was worth putting your life into it. I'm not so sure it's true anymore in this country. It is true in other countries, but not here."

Still, for all that disquietude, Miller still writes plays and will continue writing them. "It's what used to be called a bent," he noted. "It's the way my mind was formed. I think a playwright in some part is an actor; he's an actor who wants to act all the parts. You could call it a deformation of the mind, which is the way one thinks in terms of scenes, rather than descriptions. I have thought that way since I began thinking."

And this bent, as he puts it, extends to the way he writes dialogue, the intuitive sense he has of knowing that words that may read well might not always perform well when spoken on a stage, and vice versa.

"No question, there is a mystery about it," Miller said. "The only thing I can tell you about it is that, usually, a stage-worthy line invites the audience to complete it somehow. To complete the image. You see, the best theater is the theater that invokes the imagination of the audience. And it's a difficult art because there's a question of how much to tell them, how much they should be asked to work at it.

And a line—a good dramatic line—may say a lot, but it also leaves out a lot. And I can't be any more specific than that. The narrative dialogue obviously does more, but it doesn't have the kick that any dramatic dialogue does."

What is of paramount importance, he continued, is that performers and audience alike realize that good dramatic dialogue is never truly realistic. "One of the reasons *Death of a Salesman* is so successful is because it gives people real emotion; it invokes real emotion," he said. "And the truth of the matter is that the dialogue is not tape-recording dialogue. It takes good actors to realize that, and the actors know it best. So that the seeming realism of the play is created by a very highly condensed, highly selective use of language, which is not realistic speech. If it were more realistic speech, the play would be seven hours long."

One of the great criticisms generally put forth about the latest generation of American playwrights is that very few of them develop the kinds of characters Miller and the late Tennessee Williams are so famous for having created.

"I don't know why that is," Miller said. "I think maybe the idea of having some autonomous human being is strange to a lot of people now. I often wonder whether the theater's reflecting a feeling among the public that characters don't matter anymore, that we're so predetermined as to what we're going to do that psychology's boring, and it really doesn't matter what you think or what you feel. What matters is what the social circumstance is, what your job is, what you have to do and what you're forbidden to do by your job. So what we're getting maybe is a reflection back from the stage and from the movies of what we really feel. That would be pretty awful, but I often wonder whether that's the case, that today's plays are just describing man as he really thinks he is."

It comes as no surprise, then, to learn that despite a lifetime spent working in the theater, Miller considers himself outside the theater. "To tell you the truth, I've never felt that I was inside it. I've always been on the outside, and I don't regret that. As I explained, most of the plays I've written have been rejected by the critics when they were first performed. Actually, *All My Sons* would have closed shortly after it opened in New York if it hadn't have been for one critic, Brooks Atkinson of the *New York Times*, who championed it. Had he not put up a fight for it, I don't think it would have run a month. He wrote about four essays on it, and he beat down the opposition to it. Without that, and without his belief in me, I doubt that I would have had any success in the theater at all."

Death is so central to much of his work, the question arose whether Miller considers himself a writer of tragedy. "Well, death certainly is a condition that applies to all of us; however I've found in recent years that it moves away from the center of my work. And I suspect it's because I get closer to it with each decade and—I don't know—I think that in the future, something I'm working on now maybe, will complete the circle back to the tragic mode again. But it's hard to rationalize these things. I work by instinct a lot. I'm not a philosopher. I follow my nose, as *Timebends* indicates. As you can see from that book, I haven't laid out a plot; it's instructive."

Although he never lays out a plot, he added, he always insists on having one in his work. "But it discovers itself," he pointed out. "It's never preordained." If the work doesn't develop with a specific beginning, middle, and end, "then I don't complete it; it stays in the notebook, because a play without an end is not a play. It's something that's not quite born."

And once a play is abandoned, Miller never returns to it. "I can't redo something. I have to go at it fresh and get the excitement of a fresh discovery," he said. "If I'm not moved, then I can't make anybody else see anything or feel anything. It's my excitement that I have to convey."

Toni Morrison

Interviewed in Boston on March 18, 1981, for Tar Baby; *Morrison was awarded the Nobel Prize for Literature in 1993.*

With *Tar Baby*, Toni Morrison decided that, for a change, she'd take an honest stab at writing a book with a happy ending. "I tried to make this a novel in which the sun sets and everybody goes off holding hands," she said in a recent Boston interview. "I wanted a situation where various social, sexual, and racial relationships were at play, and they would be resolved because people would transcend those limitations and love one another honestly and generously." Then, Toni Morrison let out a wonderfully infectious, deep-from-the-belly laugh.

"Of course, that's what I thought I would write in the beginning," she quickly added. "The resolution, as it turned out, is unsettling because it does not reassure us about some of the things that we would like to believe in, things which we would like to believe work."

What happened, then, from the time she started to the time she finished? "My characters became fully imagined," she said. "Once that happens, I move them around, I see what feels right for them. There are certain things they just won't do, and I can't make them say things or do things that aren't natural for them."

And so, *Tar Baby*—just published by Alfred A. Knopf—ends on a disquieting note, but not mutely or without power. There is a sunset, to be sure, and the key characters know more about themselves than they did at the outset. But, as Morrison said, there is no holding hands and little reassurance. Yet—like any serious work of the imagination—it leaves its reader with an afterglow of insight.

It is true, as John Irving pointed out in his *New York Times* review, that *Tar Baby* is a black novel and a woman's novel. Morrison is a black woman who excels in the creation of female characters, and she does develop themes with strong racial motifs. But it is unfair and misleading to place any kind of label on her fiction. Her characters are too human and too complicated to be categorized by race or sex; her stories are too provocative and too resonant to suggest a limited readership.

If anything, there is a classical quality to her writing. Her characters may be energized with monumental virtues, but they're also beset with monumental flaws, which means that, typically, there is a catharsis that follows. *Tar Baby* is Morrison's fourth novel, and her first to present white characters in major roles along with blacks. Her first three novels—*The Bluest Eye*, *Sula*, and *Song of Solomon* (winner of the National Book Critics Circle award in 1977)—explored various levels of the black American experience. In addition to her splendid characterizations, her work is distinctive for the captivating settings she creates and a technique that culls a rich legacy of folklore, art, and tradition.

The major action in *Tar Baby* takes place on the verdant Caribbean island of Isle des Chevaliers. There, Valerian Street, a wealthy, decidedly eccentric white man is trying to live out his retirement in idyllic splendor. His wife, Margaret—a one-time Miss Maine, twenty years his junior—remains with him part of the year, but not without resentment.

Attending the Streets as cook and butler are Ondine and Sydney Childs, two blacks who have spent their adult lives waiting on Valerian, seemingly without reservations or complications. Their niece, Jadine—an orphan who received a Sorbonne education at

Valerian's expense—is a house guest on the island when the story opens. Jadine also is a bewitchingly beautiful woman who modeled in Paris and is considering marriage to a wealthy white man in France. She has embraced, in short, the values and goals of her white benefactors.

For a while, everything seems fine, at least on the surface. But then a new element enters the equation, one that produces an explosive reaction: Son, a retrograde seaman, finds his way to the island house and enters everyone's lives. He is unkempt and uneducated, very rough around the edges, and the antithesis of Jadine. Yet, they are attracted to each other, and a tempestuous love affair develops.

But before that happens, there is an unforgettable gathering of all the principals for a Christmas dinner. It is a priceless scene conceived in the tradition of a comedy of manners. At one end of the table, you have Valerian, the pedigreed aristocrat, at the other end is Son, the man who came in from the swamp. On either side are the former Miss Maine, Jadine, and the devoted servants who are sitting down to dinner for the first time with their employers. Before the meal is over, we learn something fundamentally revealing about everyone there.

The action moves from Isle des Chevaliers to New York to the backwoods of North Florida where Son grew up. But it is on the enchanted island where Morrison, like Shakespeare's Prospero, waves her magic wand and makes things happen. It is a place where the natural world not only lives, but mutely observes and passes judgment like a Greek chorus. It is a place where clouds gather, stand still, and watch "the river scuttle around the forest floor," where trees sigh and sway and murmur, where bees "are fat and lazy, curious about nothing," where at noon "parrots sleep and diamondbacks work down the trees toward the cooler undergrowth."

The Uncle Remus story of the tar baby works its way in with subtlety. "I've always been haunted by that story," Morrison said. "I always looked at the tar baby as a black woman. The story has a farmer—a white farmer—making the tar baby to trap a rabbit, which is obviously black and which has been eating his cabbages. Her destiny, in other words, was to entrap her brother, and that just seemed to me to be prophecy as well as history."

When she started the novel, Morrison said she did so to see "what sparks would fly" when "a black woman with sensibilities provided by white civilization meets somebody from the briar patch. In the beginning, I hoped she would go off into the briar patch with him, but as you see, it just isn't possible."

Leonard Nimoy

Interviewed in Boston on October 13, 1995, for I Am Spock.

It isn't often that an actor's personal life is profoundly shaped by a single fictional character, especially one who lives in the twenty-third century, comes from another planet, and is readily identified by a pair of pointed ears that pop up comically on both sides of his head.

Twenty years ago, when Leonard Nimoy was forty-five and still fashioning his career, he found that the half-human, half-Vulcan character he had played with such beguiling ease on the hit television series *Star Trek* was so distracting to his professional image that he brazenly titled a volume of reflections *I Am Not Spock*.

Two decades later, with a variety of assignments for television, the movies, and the stage successfully behind him, Nimoy finally is at peace not only with himself, but with his alter ego, so much so that he has titled his new autobiography *I Am Spock*.

"It took a long time for me to come to that title," Nimoy said with good-natured ease during a recent visit to Boston, the city where he grew up as the second son of a Jewish barber who had escaped persecution in Russia.

"It's comfortable for me to say that I am Spock now because I don't think there's any more division between me and the character. I think it's all gone away. Let me also say that the earlier title was not really a disclaimer, although I must have been going through some kind of complex process at the time, perhaps unconsciously. That title had some merit then because it was a fact—I was not Spock, I was Leonard Nimoy."

Disclaimer or not, Nimoy now acknowledges that *I Am Not Spock* was an unfortunate choice of titles, especially since 1975—the year that book was published—was the precise time that the *Star Trek* episodes he had made from 1966 to 1968 with William Shatner as Captain Kirk were becoming a cultural phenomenon in television reruns.

"My timing was disastrous," Nimoy agreed. "All of a sudden, there was a clamor for more *Star Trek*, and millions of people were persuaded to believe that the series ended because I had rejected Spock. The series ended when it did because of mediocre ratings; it caught fire only after it went into syndication."

A degree of redemption came for Nimoy with production of several epic motion pictures, all featuring the same characters from the television series. In addition to playing the wryly rational Mr. Spock, he directed *Star Trek III* and *Star Trek IV*, which he cowrote, and he produced *Star Trek VI*.

Also providing blessed balance to his resume have been appearances as Tevye in a touring production of *Fiddler on the Roof* and King Arthur in a revival of *Camelot*. Behind the camera, he directed the hit comedy *Three Men and a Baby* in 1987 and *The Good Mother* in 1988. He has earned several Emmy nominations, including one for his performance as Morris Meyerson opposite Ingrid Bergman in the television movie *A Woman Called Golda*.

Now, at sixty-five, Nimoy said he is pleased with what he has accomplished. "For a guy who considers himself pretty much having done the job, I find myself more busy than I want to be. I'm coproducing a television series, *Deadly Games*, and I'm working on a novel, my first, a science-fiction thriller."

It is this versatility, he said, that has contributed in large measure to the equilibrium he now maintains with his signature character. "I am more Spock-like today than I was when I started out. I've become more rational, I'm much more comfortable within my own skin. Spock always knew who he was, had a great sense of himself, had a great sense of security. I was a much more driven, more needful person. I was growing up. There were still unanswered questions for me back then."

Nimoy said he has given considerable thought to what has enabled *Star Trek* to endure through the years. "We had a family of characters that the audience enjoyed revisiting," he explained. "We were viewed as a group of professional people working in unison to solve problems. The society we represented still had a clear perception of the difference between right and wrong and knew what had to be done."

During our interview in the Ritz-Carlton café, Nimoy demonstrated—much to the delight of onlookers at nearby tables—the four-fingered, three-pronged hand sign he originated for Mr. Spock early in the television series, a gesture invariably accompanied by the words, "Live long and prosper."

"It was something I remembered seeing as an eight-year-old kid in our orthodox synagogue," he said, pointing vaguely toward the West End of Boston where he grew up. "It is a hand sign that is used during the High Holiday services when a group of priests known as Kohanim come forward and bless the congregation. Everyone is supposed to bow their heads and look away, because God's presence is being invoked. But I was curious and I peeked anyway."

Many years later, when Nimoy was trying to develop a distinctive personality for Spock, he thought, "Wouldn't it be wonderful if we had some special thing that Vulcans do when they greet?" It was then that the "magic moment" in the synagogue of his youth came to mind.

"There's no trick to it at all," Nimoy said, demonstrating the hand salute once again. "It is an acquired talent—perfected with years of diligent practice."

Edna O'Brien

Interviewed in Cambridge, Massachusetts, on May 19, 1997, for Down by the River.

I've heard that this novel is inspired by an actual case, is that true?

Not quite, no. The seed of it was perhaps sparked off in my mind, but it was not inspired for several reasons. First of all the X case—what we call the X case—this case which the whole world was in arms about, was about a girl in Dublin and she was pregnant by a friend of her father's. She went to England to have an abortion and the attorney general called her home because she was under age. I, of course, read it, and I was shocked and sorry for everyone in it. I couldn't, however, write a book—no one could—just from the newspaper article. It would have to have an inner momentum that would be quite independent of that. It is an incest story, and I wouldn't do it for the sake of sensation. I wrote it because there was something resonant in there for me. But I wasn't ready to write about it immediately. You are never ready to write a book until you are ready.

Did you find it intimidating, or at least frustrating, to see so many books out there involving the incest theme?

One writes by oneself in a far away country, and I am a little bit aware of it now with all the different books out. But again, that would be something accidental. This book took me three years to write.

I read an interview with you where it was suggested that this might be the second book of a trilogy. Is that true?

Yes, that is the case. One is the *House of Splendid Isolation*, which is about an IRA man in Ireland, and he takes a woman hostage. *Down by the River* is about a girl who is forced to carry her father's child. She is strained in every case, to put it mildly, psychologically. And a third book, which I will be beginning when I return home—please God—after all these journeys, is prompted—prompted, more than inspired, is perhaps the best word—by a murder over land. People can very desperately cling to their little bits and pieces of land, even if it is only a little field as big as an armchair. It will be the third book, and it is called *Wild Decembers* from a line in a poem of Emily Brontë's, "fifteen wild Decembers." It will be my story of Ireland at the end of this century, kind of the pulse of things that have happened there in the country, because I write about the country and I am from the country.

Did you visualize a trilogy from the beginning?

Well, I didn't at first because it is a little bit like sleep-walking. You don't really know what you are doing except that you move into a strange and unknown path. I didn't realize it until four or five years ago, until I sat down to write *House of Splendid Isolation*. It just seemed to me that one rose out of the other.

You have spent most of your adult life in London, is that right?

That is a bit of a fallacy. I live sometimes in London and quite a lot in Ireland. And I spend a good bit of time and will be spending a good bit more in New York, since I will be teaching at NYU. I have always come to New York as what is known as a visitor. But I will now be living there next year. I like to move around a bit, because for writing you have to have privacy. Now you can have that anywhere, you can have that in a city just as much as in the country, but what it mainly entails is that you can't have much of a social life. It is ironic that writers are supposed to depict the human condition and at the same time they have to be homeless. It is very funny actually.

Do you consider yourself an expatriate writer?

No, I don't go in for those words, to tell you the truth. I am a writer whose stories are rooted in my native land.

But you mentioned how on the one hand you are always expected to describe the human condition while also being required to withdraw from it. Do you find that distance sharpens your perception of your native land?

Distance always sharpens perception, but distance can just be—as Emily Dickinson would be the first to admit—just going into a room. You don't have to geographically go a million miles away to another latitude. I think that what a writer has to be—what one becomes—is ever watchful of every place, every sensation, every smell, every sound, and when you are there in a place, they renew themselves into your mind and into your memory. I wrote some of *Down by the River* in England; I wrote some of it in the west of Ireland; I wrote a good deal of it back and forth.

Is human nature a constant, in your view?

Do you mean universal?

Yes.

Absolutely. Yes, sure. The only reason—I would say the most fundamental reason—that I write about Ireland is that it is the place I know. If I set a story in Boston or Vermont or anywhere else, it wouldn't have that authenticity. Hemingway said a very intelligent thing once, he said you have to know everything, and then you have to select the things to put in. And it is not just the dialogue, the ear for the rhythms of the speech; it is the landscape, the culture, the psychological ethos. It is the history. It is everything.

You were a banned writer in Ireland at one point.

I was.

Could you describe that experience?

It has enormous repercussions. It makes one, or did to me at the time, feel secretly that I must have done something wrong, that there was some criminality in what I did. Maybe there is a criminality in any writing that is good. The trouble, I think, with present time, and something I deeply regret and lament, is that I do not have as many readers as I would like because the passion and the habit of reading is diminished, reduced greatly. People go to rock concerts or look at videos or look at television, so that maybe a bit of banning is helpful. I think the deepest crush about it is being misunderstood or punished by your own people, whom you have written about, not to parody them or humiliate them. I think that hurts, because it is shortsighted.

I think you must have an idea of whom you are writing for. Are you writing for the reader in Ireland, as well as the reader here?

I never have an idea. If you had, you would go off your head. Every single person that might read my books in Ireland would respond differently. It is almost as if it would be a different book. I write for *it*, what Kierkegaard called the purity of heart. Which reader in Ireland would you be thinking of? A schoolteacher, a doctor, a nurse, a teenager, a hippie, the Protestants, the Catholics, who? I don't think like that. It would be counterproductive. Which one of them would I be wanting to get to? It is about people, who I hope have a resonance for readers wherever they may be, whether they are in Finland or Buffalo or Africa or wherever.

You have been quoted as saying that when you are writing your fiction you do tend to gravitate towards the darker self. Is that an accurate description of what you do, and if so, why is that?

I think that is true. I like dark things, whether they are by men or by women. Most of Shakespeare, the greatest plays are dark, the tragedies and the histories. Gogol is dark. Yes, I am dark. I am very glad to be.

How would you define dark?

You depict the deepest recesses of human nature, the turmoil, the torment, the ambiguity, the fear. All that would be what one would call dark.

I read where you visited Joyce's grave. Do you often make literary pilgrimages like this?

I love Joyce. He is my master; he and Faulkner are my two masters. They are the ones I read every day of my life. I happened to be in Zurich, and I went to see Joyce's grave. It was quite comic. There was an empty Guinness bottle and one dyed green—which someone must have brought for St. Patrick's Day—just thrown on the grave. It was very near the zoo. You could hear the baying of the lions and the tigers. I thought of Joyce—who was very susceptible to sound and dreaded thunder and was very frightened of it and of animals—and this constant animal sound, like a kind of mantra. There was nobody there at all. It was a very quiet day.

I don't visit many shrines. I haven't been to Faulkner's Mississippi. The inspiration really comes from their work. I was pleased to go to Joyce's grave, and I thought it was a very comic moment out of Leopold Bloom.

How do you feel holding a precious manuscript?

That is different. I saw the handwritten manuscript in the national library in Dublin of Joyce's *Portrait of the Artist*, and to actually read the lines, even though I know it very well… They had the manuscript open to the moment in *Portrait* when the boy Stephen is having a bout of nostalgia, and he's thinking about his mother at home in her felt slippers. They let me read for a few minutes, and I did feel that it carried much more emotion reading it in his handwriting.

Perhaps we could talk about how a novel takes on a life of its own? We discussed how this new novel was sparked by an actual event.

Indeed it does. I always start with the first few lines in any book: "Ahead of them the road runs in a long entwined undulation of mud, patched tar and fjords of green, the grassy surfaces rutted and trampled, but the young shoots surgent in the sun…" At the beginning of *Down by the River*, I wanted to start to cast a kind of spell of lushness and beauty, beauty of nature, and within it a warning of something dark and dangerous. When it says they walk away, the father and daughter, and the sound of the "traffic growing fainter and fainter, a clackety river beyond, and in the odd gusts of wind the undersides of the larches purling up to show ballroom skirts of spun silver. The road silent and somnolent, yet with a speech of its own, speaking back to them, father and child, through trappings of sun and fretted verdure, speaking of the old mutinies and a fresh crime mounting in the blood."

You have to build and, in the best sense of the word, enchant the reader. So, yes, you make a novel, and you also hope to create a whole world, not just a girl and her father and their story. It is the whole community, it is the lives and the hypocrisy and the betrayals and the friendships, the different things that people are composed of. There is a proverb in the north of England where they say, "There is nothing as strange as people." So you have to create that world, the world in this book down by the river, the world of judiciary, the judges, the guards, the religious people in that community who are both religious and also compassionless, the pro-life, the pro-choice, just the whole caboodle of life.

You mentioned creating a world, and you also mentioned how great an admirer you are of the works of Faulkner. Are you creating a world not unlike his Yoknapatawpha County, in Mississippi?

Well I would like to think I am. I keep to the same place in Ireland in my fiction. I think the resemblance would be the turbulence that Faulkner talked about, the blood boiling through the land. I feel the same about the Ireland that I know, which is different from the Ireland that any other Irish writer might know or write about, very different. It is the sensibility of the writer that selects, distorts, metamorphosizes, you name it, that world to bring it to the page. Another way you could put it is like this: The Dublin that James Joyce treated both in *Dubliners* and in *Portrait* and above all in *Ulysses* is not Dublin. It is Joyce's Dublin, and it is more real to me than the city that I lived in and worked in and got on and off buses in, and fell in love in and wept in, and that's what literature does. That's what Faulkner does, that's what Joyce does. They totally create a fictional, mythical, totally convincing, archetypal world that happens also to bear some relation to a real world. But you have to have the two. Unless you have the archetypal reach or breadth, the books are short lived.

Do you have an anxiety about the future of the novel? Is it going to be able to keep doing the kinds of things that you just described?

I think, to tell you the truth, there are an awful lot of clever books. A book has to have soul as well brilliance. The soul is the feeling. I am sure there are women and men in parts of Africa who have great stories to tell and great language in which to tell them, but we don't know about them. I think a lot of Western fiction is slightly dated. A writer I do admire, an American writer who creates a landscape, is Cormac McCarthy. I admire him. Beckett said a great thing about writing—he was talking about James Joyce—he said it is very easy to write, you just have to make the words do the work. And Cormac McCarthy does let the words do the work. I admire his work. I can see in it some real bravura as well.

It is a restless and careless world, and there are so many books. Everyone is clamoring. And also there is that terrible thing called fashion. Certain kinds of reading are more fashionable than others. But you have to stay the course. The horse that stays the course is the one that wins the race.

Paperback editions of Oe's other works of fiction—*A Personal Matter* (1968), *Teach Us to Outgrow Our Madness* (1977), and *The Crazy Iris and Other Stories* (1977)—are available from Grove Press. An English-language edition of *The Silent Cry* (1974) is available from Kodansha International.

Nip the Buds, Shoot the Kids has autobiographical overtones, drawing on the author's childhood in a rural community on the island of Shikoku during the Second World War. In the book, fifteen boys are evacuated to a remote village much like the one the writer knew as a child.

"I wanted to write what I was feeling as a boy in this small village that is surrounded by a thick, dense forest," he said. "I was educated under a very strong imperialist creed. Every morning the teacher would ask, 'If the Great God Emperor asks you to die, then you must say you will die.' But sometimes I hesitated to say, 'Yes, I will die.' I could not believe that the Great God Emperor even knew my name or of my existence in this place."

The war and its legacy, and the U.S. occupation of Japan, are principal themes in Oe's early writing. Yet a personal tragedy—the birth of a son with a herniated brain in 1963—shaped his later work.

Advised by doctors to let the boy die, Oe and his wife, Yukari, authorized surgery that saved Hikari but left him severely disabled. Oe's decision to proceed with the operation was made days after he visited Hiroshima and spoke to survivors.

"The reality is that I went to Hiroshima to avoid making the decision," Oe said. "I was escaping from the reality of my baby. But what I found in Hiroshima was a great new image of the human being that changed my life."

Since then, each of Oe's books has explored the meaning of his son's experience and weighed the effect it has had on his own life. Particularly rewarding has been a remarkable development: the emergence of his son as a composer of unusual music for piano and flute.

Kenzaburo Oe

*Interviewed in Boston on May 1, 1995,
for* Nip the Buds, Shoot the Kids.

Shortly after the Japanese writer Kenzaburo Oe won last year's Nobel Prize in literature, he announced he would not publish anything for five years. The sixty-year-old author said he would spend the time immersed in study, then strive to create a new type of narrative form.

"What I want to do is to create the conclusion of my own literature," he said recently in Cambridge, Massachusetts. "For this endeavor, I must study, I must read some philosophy and some other novelists. I want to think deeply, then I want to understand the true meaning of my life, my generation, my place."

The Nobel Prize stipend of about $930,000 gives Oe (OH-ay) the independence to pursue other avenues of literary expression. The irony is that the award enables him to take a sabbatical from writing just as it heightens interest in his work.

In the United States, two of Oe's books have just been released by British publisher Marion Boyars in new, English-language editions: *Nip the Buds, Shoot the Kids*, his first novel, was written in 1958, establishing his reputation as a writer of consequence; and *Hiroshima Notes*, a collection of essays on the meaning of the atomic-bomb attack on his country fifty years ago, was first published in 1965.

through different borders of the city, of the inner self, and therefore of the story. Each book is like a stepping stone to the next book. It is a very unconscious process. Writing is very unconscious. If you were to plan, it wouldn't be very good at all. You look deeper into things with each book, because you have to dredge deeper. The first book is always the easiest. It is waiting in the wings of your mind to be written, if you happen to be a writer. The eighth or ninth or fifteenth book, because the landscape is the same, the people have maybe multiplied but some of their passions and their obsessions are rooted in that same place. So you can't tell that same old story. You have to give it a new dynamic. But they are still cousins. It is a tribe.

Have you ever been tempted to rewrite any of your earlier books?

Most of my books speak for who I was at that particular time. There is one book I did not realize as fully or as organically as I feel I could have. It was called *The High Road*. It didn't have that cathartic effect, that emotional effect. If I were writing it today, I would certainly improve it. But I am never tempted to go back because I have too much to do.

If I had access to the men who run the big television networks, I would every night before the shock of the TV news read a piece of text for five minutes, no more. The Bible, a piece of Gospel, a piece of Shakespeare, a poem of Emily Dickinson, a paragraph of Faulkner, whatever it would be. Great stuff, and I honestly think it would bestir people, because when you read a book—just as when you are writing a book, except writing a book takes longer—there is no doubt about it, you reach a deeper part of your own self. Now it is a restless world, and it is a crowded world. People are tired. They are tired from everything. To concentrate, to even sit and concentrate and read two pages, that's all you need to do. You don't even need to read a complete work. Even if it is just a sonnet. Just before a reading the other day, I read a poem of Emily Dickinson that was taped to the wall, and it was wonderful. A beautiful poem, and the idea was that hope is like a feather that touches you. She was fantastic, Emily Dickinson. My other great hero from these parts is Sylvia Plath. She knew what she was doing, a great poet.

Let's talk about narratives. There must be a point at which storytelling takes center stage for you?
Let there be no mistake about it. If you think about the great books down the years, the story has to move with inevitable and ever-gripping momentum. The pulse of the story moves. All great books must have a sense of a story being told.

You have also written children's books. I must assume that children are a very important readership to you?
They are. Prisoners and children would be the most captive audience.

Is every book part of a corpus for you?
It would be the way one's arms are part of one's body. Everything is a continuum. What happens is the books in my own case become more labyrinthine. You are in the same universe, but you are breaking

Oe used to carry Hikari on his shoulders in the woods and point out various animals. "We had a recording that we played over and over for him—the sounds of bird songs," he said. "One day, he began chirping the songs of various birds; soon he knew the songs of seventy different birds. We started to play recordings of Bach and Mozart for him, and before long he could identify these pieces as well."

Hikari Oe's two compact discs have enjoyed great success in Japan. For a while, the father believed that his mission was to write lyrics for his son's music—but he has since abandoned the idea.

"I was thinking that, since my son cannot express himself in words, perhaps I should be his interpreter. But I find now I was mistaken: My son can understand himself in his music." The lesson is clear, Oe said. "If my son can create music, I must also do something for my spirit, for my soul."

He hopes to "explore the possibility" of a new form of literature. "I hope to create a concentrated style. It will not be a novel or a short story or an essay. It will include everything I know. And it is important that I talk to everyone. I hope to write some works which can be read by children and by old people alike. It is my gift for the twenty-first century."

Grace Paley

*Interviewed in Cambridge, Massachusetts,
on May 7, 1994, for* The Collected Stories.

When Grace Paley began to write powerful stories about women's lives in the 1950s, she had no idea that her work would one day be praised by literary historians for its innovative themes, lyrical beauty, and insight into the human soul.

"Me, a pioneer?" the seventy-one-year-old New York native said with an incredulous laugh during an interview in Cambridge in which she discussed her life as a writer of note and consequence.

"I started to write because I had things I wanted to put down on paper, that's all," she continued. "I began to think about people I knew. I had some deep concerns, and something very real inside of me—call it internal pressure, if you want—moved me to start writing."

A first-generation daughter of Russian-Jewish immigrants who now lives in Vermont, Paley grew up in the Bronx surrounded by a variety of rich ethnic voices and cultural dialects. Sometime around 1954 or 1955, when she and her first husband were living in Greenwich Village with their two young children, the first stories began to emerge from this state of creative tension. "I had always written poems, but with no idea that I was going to ever publish them," she recalled. "I started to think about stories around the same time I began to think about women's lives. There were a lot of women in the Village then, living by themselves."

Many were divorced, others were merely alone. "Some of them had been dumped, a lot of them had children, and they were all very interesting to me. I became very worried, very upset, and that's when I started to write."

She had no illusions, however, about whether any of her stories would ever be published. "This was a very masculine period in literature, and here I was writing a story about three spinster aunts. I said to myself, 'Nobody's going to be interested in these stories about a bunch of women.'"

Not surprisingly, Paley's first queries to magazines were answered with letters of rejection. One day, the former husband of a friend who lived in the same apartment building approached her while visiting his children and said he wanted to read some of her work.

"His name was Ken McCormick, and he was a senior editor at Doubleday," Paley said. "His ex-wife, Tibby, told him he had to read them. I gave him three stories. A couple of weeks later, he came back and said, 'Write seven more like the three you gave me, and I'll publish them in a book.'"

Her first collection, *The Little Disturbances of Man*, was published in 1959, and McCormick's enthusiasm for her work is evident on the inside dust jacket of the book, first editions of which are dearly coveted today by collectors. This is part of what he wrote: "Grace Paley is one of the most original and talented young writers we have ever published. This is a flat-footed statement—but we hold to it because we feel these ten extraordinary short stories will make Grace Paley one of the most talked-about writers of the season."

That collection, and the two others that followed, *Enormous Changes at the Last Minute* (1974) and *Later the Same Day* (1985), have now been gathered into a single volume, titled simply *The Collected Stories*. The forty-five pieces reflect Paley's development as a writer during five eventful decades of American life, yet her sharp sense of humor and ear for engaging dialogue are consistent throughout. Especially remarkable is how she accomplishes so much in so few words.

"One thing Ken did," Paley said, "he told me I should write a novel. So I wrote one. I worked on a novel for two years, but it wasn't any good. I had brains enough to know that it was crummy. I used parts of it in different stories, but most of it I threw out."

The principal flaw with the longer narrative form, she decided, was that what she was doing was too imitative. "And I had no idea what I was imitating. It was like I lost my ears and my voice, as well as my brains. It wasn't there. So I write stories."

Most of the women she writes about are imaginary, though one character, Faith Darwin, appears periodically in each of the three collections, and comes as close as any to Grace Paley herself, right down to the similarity of the first names. "I've allowed her to have one or two of my experiences. When I start writing in the first person, it usually involves Faith."

The genesis of any story, Paley said, typically comes with something she hears. "It usually starts with someone saying something. I hear something, and I start to write. Then what happens is that I put it down on paper and don't look at it again for a long time." Sometimes, a year may pass before she returns to a piece she has written. "Usually, when I write something down the first time, it's all wrong. I have to do a lot more work before I get it right. Sometimes you write down half a story, half a paragraph, a page maybe, and you still haven't said what you mean. I just keep at it until I feel I have it right."

Paley said the idea that she was breaking ground for other writers never occurred to her forty years ago. "My feeling now is that back in the Fifties and early Sixties, we were just accumulating drops that made a wave. I knew by the end of my first book that I was a feminist, but I didn't know I was a feminist when I started."

While delighted to see the body of her work gathered in one volume, Paley said she was uneasy at first about going back and getting everything together. "I'm so scared to look at it, even now," she said. "I guess I'm scared because maybe I'll get too much of an idea of what I'm about. You know what I mean? I thought, you know, that was then, this is now. But I'm glad I did it because it made me feel more open, in a way that surprises me, to what comes next."

Mario Puzo

Interviewed in New York City on July 24, 1996, for The Last Don.

There was a time back in the 1950s when two up-and-coming New York novelists—Mario Puzo, from a rough West Side neighborhood known as Hell's Kitchen, and Joseph Heller, of Coney Island, in Brooklyn—would get together to play cards with friends and dream out loud about fame and fortune.

Those were the days when determined young authors used such phrases as "serious fiction" to describe their creative objectives, and "selling out" to disparage others who disdained "real literature" to write books that might one day become runaway bestsellers.

Puzo was the first of the pair to break into print, with the release in 1955 of *The Dark Arena*, a tightly crafted novel that drew a flurry of positive reviews but sold sparsely all the same. Nine years later his next book, a chronicle of Italian immigrant life titled *The Fortunate Pilgrim*, was greeted with similar enthusiasm—"a small classic," the *New York Times* declared—but recorded sales just as paltry.

"I published those two novels, and I was poorer than when I started out," Puzo recalled during an interview in the penthouse suite of a Fifth Avenue hotel overlooking Central Park.

Our conversation was occasioned by publication of *The Last Don*, Puzo's seventh book, which has just been issued in a first printing of 350,000 copies, a telling indication of just how profoundly circumstances have changed over the past four decades for the seventy-five-year-old author. Indeed, his most triumphant effort of all, *The Godfather*, has registered sales of 21 million copies worldwide since its release twenty-seven years ago. But that's getting ahead of the story.

Early in 1961, Puzo was the published author, and Joseph Heller was still a hopeful aspirant. By the end of the year, *Catch-22*—Heller's first book and by far his best known—convincingly proved that success and critical acclaim are possible in one fell swoop; it also prompted Puzo to take notice of what had happened.

"I grew up believing that if you published a novel, you automatically became rich and famous, especially if the novel got good reviews," Puzo said. "Well, I got terrific reviews, and I couldn't even get a paperback house to pick up my second book." And that, he emphasized, is what annoyed him more than anything else.

"I had been bragging all along to my family and my friends that I could write a bestseller whenever I wanted to, but I wouldn't demean myself to do that, and I certainly would never sell a book to the movies. I was young, you know? Everybody wanted to be a great writer. The biggest insult you could say to a guy back then was, 'You're nothing, you write for the movies.'"

What Puzo did next was to discard everything he had learned in literature courses at City College, which he attended under the G.I. Bill after an uneventful tour overseas in the U.S. Army during the Second World War, and at the New School for Social Research in Greenwich Village, "where everyone went" who wanted to be a "great" writer and where he met Heller.

"I was taught that there should be nothing extraneous about a novel," he said. "Even if you write something really good, the rule was you should cut it out if it isn't absolutely necessary. So I did that in my first two books. But in *The Godfather* I threw *everything* in, maybe because it was funny, maybe because it was exciting, or just because I liked it. If I thought it was good, I kept it in. So I came piece by piece to writing a bestseller."

What Puzo modestly envisioned from this admittedly commercial venture was "to make maybe a hundred grand," a veritable fortune in those days. "Believe me," he said, "I had no idea that all this was going to happen."

Looking back at precisely what made "all this" possible—the string of blockbuster books, the Academy Award–winning movies, the palatial estate on Long Island—Puzo now believes it was that he wrote "an American fairy tale," even if the principal characters involved are ruthless gangsters who populate an underworld subculture known as the Mafia.

"I am not a realistic novelist," he stressed. "*The Godfather* is a romantic novel and this new book is a romantic novel as well. They're both family novels; I think of each one as a family novel where the family business happens to be against the law."

In *The Last Don*, Puzo brings the affairs of the "family business" into the immediate present, with the current godfather, Domenico Clericuzio, making plans to legitimize all operations. Echoes of *The Godfather*, which began with a wedding, are apparent in *The Last Don*, which opens with the 1965 christening of two cousins who will be at the center of the bloody turmoil that develops.

While the Clericuzio interests are based in New York, the focus is largely on the high-stakes workings of the Hollywood film industry and the Las Vegas gambling casinos, two worlds Puzo knows intimately, and which he profiles with uncommon wit and insight. Dozens of wonderfully developed characters enliven the novel, and there is a genuinely surprising ending that is virtually impossible to predict.

"I knew the two books would be compared," Puzo said, "but so what? I was writing what I knew would be another book, so it didn't make any difference to me. This is the world I know best, even if most of it is all made up."

The true irony of his celebrity as an authority on the underworld, he explained, is that the most memorably "authentic" details in his

Mafia books are inventions. In *The Last Don*, for instance, a mob hit intended to make a victim disappear is called a "communion." A "confirmation" is when the body is supposed to be found. "I made them up," Puzo said. "That idea in *The Godfather* of offering a guy a deal he can't refuse? That's made up. Calling the head of a Mafia family a 'godfather'? I made that up."

Before Puzo gave that word this added context, "godfather" was used strictly to identify a man who sponsors a child's baptism; it did not include the nefarious nuance it also has today.

"You can look it up in your dictionary," he said while chomping on an unlit cigar. "And while you're at it, look up catch-22. That's in there, too. It's amazing, don't you think? Here you have two guys who have been friends for forty years, and each one of us gave a word to the English language that everyone knows. If you want to know the truth, that's my proudest boast."

Margret Rey

Interviewed in Cambridge, Massachusetts, on August 2, 1996, for the Curious George *series of children's books.*

Context is everything, a saying that takes on special meaning during a visit to the home of Margret Rey, a German-born writer who achieved international fame six decades ago with her late husband, the noted artist and book illustrator H. A. Rey.

In one corner of Rey's Cambridge, Massachusetts, living room is a cluster of stuffed animals, each bearing the likeness of a tailless monkey known to several generations of young readers as Curious George. On the walls are various drawings, sketches, and paintings, and scattered throughout the house are assorted trinkets, toys, and curiosities, all celebrating one antic or another of the same amiable creature.

"You must understand this is not an obsession with me at all," Rey insisted in an interview earlier this month on the eve of her ninetieth birthday. "But he is the family breadwinner; he has put food on my table for many, many years."

Now known to readers in more than a dozen languages and by numerous names (Fifi and Jorge el Curioso among them), Curious George made his debut in 1939. Total sales of his adventures now number more than 12 million copies worldwide.

Last fall, Houghton Mifflin released *The Complete Adventures of Curious George*, which has just gone into a large fourth printing. George's first appearance came as one of eight simian siblings, each the offspring of Mother Pamplemoose, who together befriend a lonesome giraffe whose friends have all gone off to the zoo. Published first in Paris, the English title of the book was *Cecily G. and the 9 Monkeys.*

"My husband had done some cartoons for Paris newspapers, and one of them was about a giraffe," Rey recalled. "At some point, Gallimard, the French publisher, called and asked if we could make a book out of the animal. Well, we had never thought of children's books, but we needed money, so we did it."

To their pleasant surprise, the Reys subsequently found themselves embarked on a new career as collaborators on a series of enormously popular books featuring a variety of charming characters. "My husband and I had no children of our own, but we always loved animals. The first thing we did when we visited a new city was go to the zoo."

As she talked about some of the pets she and her husband owned over the years—including turtles in Paris; monkeys in Brazil; alligators, chameleons, and newts at a summer home in New Hampshire—Jeannie, the latest in a long line of cocker spaniels to grace the Rey household, arrived, almost on cue, in the living room.

"Oh, she's such a baby," Rey said in heavily accented German and pointed with amusement to a training diaper secured firmly around the young dog's hind quarters. "My husband always managed to get one of our cocker spaniels somewhere in each of our books."

H. A. (Hans Augusto) Rey was born in Hamburg, Germany, in 1898, and started drawing at the age of two. After the First World War, he designed circus posters to earn extra money while studying philosophy and linguistics in Munich and Hamburg, and he learned how to lithograph his drawings directly from printing stones, a skill that proved useful years later when he was living in Paris and executing color separations for his own book illustrations.

The Reys were married in 1935 and lived in France and Brazil before settling in the United States in 1940. "With the Nazis on our heels, we left Paris on two bicycles that my husband put together from spare parts," Rey said. "I was very surprised he was able to do that; I didn't know he was so efficient. We took the few books we had made together with us, which proved to be a very sensible thing, because it showed people what we could do."

Within a week of their arrival in New York, the couple found an American home for Curious George with Houghton Mifflin. In 1963, they left their Greenwich Village apartment for a house near Harvard Square in Cambridge.

Instead of flooding the market with Curious George books, the Reys paced themselves. "People always think these little stories are effortless, but it took us an enormous amount of time to do each book, and after each book, we said, 'No more, too much trouble.' But it is like having children, I suppose; after four or five years, you have more or less forgotten the pain, and then we would do another. The trick is to make it look easy."

The work was evenly split, with H. A. doing the art and Margret the writing. In addition to their work on Curious George, they did other books, a few featuring dogs named Pretzel and Spotty. Since H. A. Rey's death in 1977, Margret Rey has carefully controlled their signature character, and signs off on all business decisions involving his use.

Since she firmly believes that all children have the same sense of wonder, Rey is not surprised by the universal appeal of the stories. "The secret, I believe, is that George does the kind of naughty things that all children love to do. He gets himself into trouble, but he always gets out of it through his own ingenuity." But that, she stressed, is just guesswork.

"The truth is that we did the stories exactly the way we liked them, that was our only limit, to please ourselves first," she said. "By happy coincidence the children seemed to like them, too."

Oliver Sacks

*Interviewed in Boston on February 22, 1995,
for* An Anthropologist on Mars.

Dr. Oliver Sacks is a clinical neurologist whose mission in life is to make sense out of human defects, disorders, and diseases. The world he probes is populated by people afflicted with such ailments as post-encephalitic Parkinsonianism, hypermnesia, cerebral achromatopsia, deafness, autism, and Tourette's syndrome, perplexing conditions that often produce a kaleidoscope of unusual behavior.

As the author of books noteworthy as much for their grace and sensitivity as they are for their wisdom and perception, Sacks ranks among physicians who have distinguished themselves in the world of letters. The elite honor roll has included François Rabelais, Anton Chekhov, Arthur Conan Doyle, W. Somerset Maugham, William Carlos Williams, Walker Percy, Michael Crichton, and Ethan Canin in fiction, drama, and poetry, and last year's winner of the National Book Award for nonfiction, Sherwin B. Nuland, for *How We Die*.

A native of England who has lived and worked in New York City as a "resident alien" for the past thirty-four years, Sacks is known to millions of filmgoers as the compassionate doctor played by Robin Williams in *Awakenings*, a movie based on his 1973 account of post-encephalitic patients who return briefly to normalcy after years of unconsciousness. That book also inspired a Harold Pinter play, *A Kind of Alaska*.

Sacks's 1988 work, *The Man Who Mistook His Wife for a Hat*, profiled the dilemma of a musician who lost the ability to identify everyday objects and was an international bestseller. A play based on the work, *L'Homme Qui...* by Peter Brook, opened March 13 at the Brooklyn Academy of Music's Majestic Theater.

Yet for all the acclaim his books have received, Sacks remains a physician motivated by a need to know as much as he can about the mysteries of life. Frequently, his investigations reach beyond the boundaries of the extreme to encompass identity, concepts of self, and the wellsprings of creativity. "I certainly don't think of myself as a literary figure," he said during an interview occasioned by release of his sixth book, *An Anthropologist on Mars*.

"I'm embarrassed and slightly annoyed when people talk about literary genres, which is never a word I use myself. For me, narrative has always been a way of organizing my own thoughts." He noted, however, that he has "had a pen and paper in hand almost since I can remember," and that his passion for writing earned him the nickname of "Inky" as a child. In a subtitle, Sacks identifies *An Anthropologist on Mars* as "seven paradoxical tales," a description he acknowledged is only partially applicable. "These seven cases were never conceived as seven related cases, these are pieces written at different times and different moods," he explained. "But I do think that in each case one sees how a life, an identity that sort of fits the condition, has been present."

In the title piece, Sacks introduces Temple Grandin, an animal behavior specialist who is unable to experience basic emotions or to enjoy interpersonal relationships. She is able to intellectualize complex emotions, but not feel them. "Most of the time," she says, "I feel like an anthropologist on Mars."

Many of his patients, Dr. Sacks said, are "just torn apart and devastated and embittered and ruined by what has happened to them. But I also see unexpected strengths and resources being called out, and at times there are aspects of the disease itself which can be positive. I think the theme of some of these unexpected 'positivities,' if you will, the possibility of drawing them out, is a theme of the book."

In "The Case of the Color-blind Painter," a man Dr. Sacks calls Mr. I., an artist of some renown, is involved in an automobile accident and suddenly finds himself unable to distinguish colors. "I don't say that this man became a better artist after losing his color," Dr. Sacks said. "But what was extraordinary was that even though there was no recovery in a neurological sense, there was a rebirth or renewal or reconstruction of his creative identity and his sensibility in the terms he now had."

Instead of letting the mishap destroy him, Mr. I. turned the loss "into a portal into a new world" by painting in black and white. Several of his works are reproduced in the book. "He regards what he now has as a privileged form of vision, because now he is more conscious of texture, of shape, of movement, of delicacy," Sacks said. "He finds himself in a refined world, and the rest of us, the so-called 'color normals,' are the ones who are distracted by something that is extraneous."

Sacks agreed that he walks a fine line whenever he decides that a patient is about to become a character in one of his books. "First of all, this doesn't happen all that often," he said, and explained that every case he has written about emerges from a conviction that he must learn as much as he can about his patients.

"I want to see the details of people's lives and to share them to some extent, if I can, without being voyeuristic or invasive or intrusive," he said. "There is this situation, as in anthropology, where you're a participant observer, but it's a delicate business, and there is always the danger of indelicacy. I never pry further than I'm welcome. I sort of wait to see what kind of space is allowed for me for penetration."

Because he writes with such sympathy for his characters, and since each, in a way, achieves a degree of equilibrium with their conditions, there is an uplifting quality to the book.

"I will agree with that assessment, but only if it is coupled with the notion that these are individuals with different ways of showing some sort of resource and courage," he said. "This is more a book of surviving tragic and horrible situations than it is of triumph."

A dedicated swimmer, Sacks agrees to go on book tours only if the hotels he is staying in are in close proximity to a pool. On the morning of our interview, he awoke at 5 A.M. and did "my 2K," a two-thousand meter swim, at a nearby Y.M.C.A.

"I do my best thinking when I'm swimming," he said. "There's some sort of calming, stimulation, freedom, and lack of self-consciousness for me when I swim. Maybe it has something to do with the rhythm, but I go into a trance-like state. I move at exactly the same rate, which is a meter a second, whether I swim for a hundred or a thousand or ten thousand meters, and I don't care whether people are going faster or slower. But there's always some sort of mystical feeling for me, and I become exceedingly anxious and a bit annoyed if I am forced for some reason to miss a day in the pool."

Neil Simon

Interviewed in his New York City apartment on September 29, 1996, for Rewrites, *an autobiography; Simon has won three Tony Awards and a Pulitzer Prize for drama.*

Rewrites is a very personal memoir, particularly when you write about your first wife, Joan, dying of cancer. How did your family react to it?

My daughter read it, and she said she read up to the last thirty pages and then couldn't go near it. But then finally she did, and she said that although she cried a lot, it was a catharsis for her, because she remembers it differently. She didn't realize what went on between me and Joan's mother and my friends, who were the other ones who got me through it. It was like a whole new experience for her. She feels like she has been filled in with a lot of information that she didn't know. She says because her sister was five years older, that she just wishes she had five years more with Joan.

I have to tell you, though, that there are some very funny lines in here.

Well, that's part of my business. But I wasn't sure I would be able to do it in prose, though I think I found a way. I think my playwriting career helped me write this book because I seem to have a natural ability, I guess, for construction, even though I don't sit down to plan the construction. But I find that whenever I write something, there usually is a beginning, a middle, and an end, even though I may deviate and go back and forth in time.

Did you rewrite this book with the same intensity that you do with your plays?

Well, not quite as much because when you do a play, you try out the play. You're trying it out night after night after night, and there are different audience reactions. And there are different critics—well not during the previews, but certainly when you're out of town. You keep adjusting it and adjusting it. Here the rewrites come mostly from when I finished the book, put it aside for a month or so, went back and started to read, and started to fix things up. Then came the process of working with the editors, who would say, "That's a wonderful story, but I think it's irrelevant to what you're saying at this point. Let's leave that out, unless you don't want to." They were very good about that.

A different experience for you, isn't it, because a playwright doesn't really have an editor?

No, you don't. The closest you come is with a director, who will only suggest. But he knows you're going to see it on stage when he sees it, and you'll both make the decision at the same time. But here I was relying a lot on what Michael Korda and Chuck Adams of Simon and Schuster had to say about it, and sometimes they would say, "You didn't go far enough with this. This is good, let's hear more about it." They wanted to know why I left out something—I can't recall what it was. So I wrote them a two-page letter telling them why I left the thing out of the book, and Chuck Adams called me back and said, "Can I put the letter in the book, because you explained exactly what I wanted to know?" So that process was wonderful. And then there are various other editors, as you know, who just clean up the copy, the grammar, the spelling, etc.

The legal review, that kind of drove me crazy. They would say, "Can you verify that your mother and father had these fights?" And

I said, "I beg your pardon, I was there." I mean, they are just so specific about things. They are so afraid. Perhaps your father is alive, and he's going to come and sue them for this.

That's ridiculous.

It is. It is.

I am just so impressed by this process of writing for performance. A play is a continual work in progress.

It is so malleable, you keep changing it.

You don't get that with a book. Once it's done…

Once it's done, right.

Would you like to go back and tinker a little bit?

I guess, sure. I have with everything I've ever written. I do go back with plays that have opened. I go back a couple months later, and I'll say, "Let's take out that speech, and let me add a different speech there. I've finally fixed it." There's a play I did, *Laughter on the 23rd Floor*, and there was an exit line that truly needed a laugh. It cried out for something funny at that moment and I never could get it. Three months later, my daughter said something to me, just switched some words around, and I was able to put it in. So it won't happen with *Rewrites*, but I'll get another chance, because there will be a sequel to this.

An obvious sequel. You say very early in the book, you love great beginnings.

Well, that's true, I do—with everything, in life, in plays. Abe Burrows, the author, said anyone can write the first act to a play. It's the second act that separates the boys from the men, or the girls from the ladies. I wrote the introduction after I finished the book, and I intended to write the full book, but when I got to around page 400, I said if I keep on writing about the next twenty years, it's another 400 pages. I don't want an 800-page book as an autobiography. It seems presumptuous on my part. I felt spent, after I wrote that twenty-five or thirty pages about Joan. I said, I just don't want to deal with it anymore. So I put it aside, and Michael Korda said, *absolutely*.

People think that because you've written so many genuinely funny things, that critics expect you to be funny all the time.

They may have in the beginning, but I think with the plays I've done in the last fifteen years, which have been much more serious plays—at least the subjects are dramatic, even though there is comedy within—they stopped expecting that with me. It's interesting. It's such a love-hate relationship. I love it when you learn something from them.

A *New York Times* reviewer really irritated me, not so much what he didn't like about *Rewrites*, because I've gotten some really wonderful reviews, but he started comparing the end of the book, my telling of the death of Joan, to the one I did in the play of *Jake's Women*. And that irritated me so much because he was now treating something that is so important to me and my family as something about commerce. Gee, I could do the ending of Joan's death better. I could make it more touching, more emotional. It's mind-boggling that somebody would be so idiotic to write something like that. But this was a man from *Variety* they got to write the review.

I mean, give me William Safire, give me John Updike. You know, if you want to knock the prose, I'll take it from them. But *Variety*? Please. The people who don't read books write hurtful reviews of them. I'm used to getting bad reviews in the theater, and you can't complain about a bad review on your play. It's not done. But I was complaining about this review—this thing of singling out how I portrayed my wife's death. You can see what a kind of mind that is, and also that he comes from *Variety*, which is not known for its prose.

I think that in drama the review is so much more important, though; it can really spell the difference between life and death.

Well, because you've only got about eight or nine that make a difference. Although I've overcome a lot of *New York Times* bad reviews. If the play is solid, and the word of mouth is good during the previews, you can overcome it, and they'll just say, "Oh, well, that critic, he always gives bad reviews." Frank Rich was the critic for the *Times* for so many years. He was called the Butcher of Broadway—with good reason, I think. He could give you a good review, and if the audiences didn't like you, they're just not going to come. So it's up to them eventually. But that's what you have to live with.

Big, based on the Tom Hanks movie, just closed with a $10 million loss. It's unbelievable. Ten million dollars for a musical! The stakes are big. I don't know where they get their money. It's very hard to get money to do a straight play, because the returns aren't as big, because you can't run eight, nine, or ten years like the *Phantom of the Opera*. If a play is a hit today, and it runs a year and a half, you've had a big hit.

I know how hard it is to publish a book for the first time; I have to think that getting a play produced is the most intimidating thing in the world. What do you tell a youngster who comes up to you and says, "I want to be a playwright"?

Well, there aren't a lot of them who come up anymore, because they're all aiming to write screenplays. And then they want to drop the screenplays and become a director. Writing films, since I came into it, has changed so much that there's hardly a writer who can make a contract and say, "I can't be rewritten. If you want rewrites I'll do it." The studios all say, "No, we want to bring in other writers," because their investment is $70 million, $80 million, something like that.

I'm amazed when I hear about someone who wants to be a playwright. I called Stanford University once, because I wanted to teach for one year. I was looking around for what universities I could go to, and I liked the idea of Stanford. It was close enough to home not to be away so long. They were overwhelmed, and they said, "My God, yes, we would love it." I said, "Well, just tell me how many students you think you'd get." She called me back in about three days and said, "We can get five." And I said, "How many if I taught screenplay writing?" She said, "Well over two hundred." So that's where the world is going.

Do you think, then, that playwriting is an anachronism?

No, I don't. But I think the writers will persist. I think people will always want live theater. The venues will change because of dollars, which is what the movie business is about. The day that I first saw in the *New York Times*, which has to be well over ten years ago, where the *New York Times* started printing the grosses each week of the movies, I said, "It's all over, because now it's all about money." It's not about how good it is. When you hear people in California talk about a picture, they rarely talk about the quality of the picture. They may say it's great or it's bad, but they never talk about what the content is about. They'll say, "It did $60 million" and "I think it could go through the roof and do $100 million." That's what they talk about.

You mentioned home. Home now for you is L.A.?

I live there mostly now because I'm married to Diane Lander, and we have a twelve-year-old daughter, and she's in school there. My two daughters live in Santa Barbara. One is writing screenplays. Nancy's writing short stories. So it's easier for me to be there. But this apartment—we've been here for eight or nine years. When I do a play, I come here, and I spend a lot of time. But New York is still home. I'm rooting for the Yankees.

Thousands and thousands of people were out there today for the festival New York is Book Country.

I know. I know. That's what's great. L.A.? No. There were some good bookstores in L.A., but you can't find them anymore.

I have to think that being a playwright is like being a musician, you know instantly if an audience likes your work or doesn't.

You know it immediately. I know it on the first night that we show it to an audience what that reaction is. It may not be totally accurate, but you can tell after that first week: This audience loves this play. It doesn't mean that the critics will, but it makes me feel good about the play. But a book? It got around to some of my friends, and what they think trickles in. You get a phone call here, you get another phone call there. It's a totally different process. I get it eventually, but it takes a long time. I'm doing a new play next summer that I've been on for five years through a lot of rewrites. Then I wrote it as a film. A number of studios wanted to buy it, and I said, "Hey, they're anxious for it, I think I'll go back and do it as a play." I had more faith in it. So I have to wait a long time until I get that first reaction.

You've been so private about yourself over the years, and although I've seen many of your plays and many of your films, I didn't realize until I read this book how much of yourself you wrote into the scripts.

I did, even though I changed the facts around a lot. For example, something like *Brighton Beach Memoirs*, which in the play has my family taking in my mother's sister and their two daughters. In real life, it was the opposite. My parents broke up and my mother and I went to live with a cousin, and my brother went to live with an aunt. And so I'm not interested in making these plays autobiographical so that you know what my life's about.

But the process is there, that you are taking elements from your own life.

Yes, I have to. I've done it in about nine of the twenty-nine plays I've done.

That's a lot.

I think so, yes. But what I consider autobiographical isn't even about me—*The Odd Couple* was about my brother and a good friend of ours. Sometimes I can make a mistake in geography and not get the play right. For example, I wrote a play that was not very successful and that I didn't like very much. It was called *Star-Spangled Girl*. Had I set it in New York, it would have been a better play, because I would know where the people went to and where they came back. I was writing about San Francisco where I had never been. It's like writing in a vacuum, and it's absolutely wrong for me.

I did a play as part of *London Suite* [a set of four one-act plays] about two Englishmen, a writer and his business manager who robbed him of all his money, and he brings him up to this hotel to kill him, and ultimately he doesn't, he just humiliates him. It was tough going here because I was keeping so close to the English idiom, which I can write sometimes well. But had I made that an American play, it would have been much better.

Do you have a sense of whom you're writing for, who the audience is?

It depends on what medium I'm writing for. I have no sense if I write for television, none. It's 22 million people out there. They could be in a garage someplace drinking beer, and I have no idea what they want to see, and it's generally not what I want to write. With a movie, it comes down to the numbers, but again that's spread out over the country. When I think about my plays, I don't think where the opening will be, I'll think of New York. One thousand people in the theater that night, and a tough audience, and if it goes well there, I feel that I've done well with it. So that's who I picture. I can picture some of the critics, but that's pointless because you can never outguess the critics.

Do you make yourself laugh? Do you have to think it's funny?

When I'm writing it, at the moment that it happens, some things will make me laugh, others I just like. There was a time when I would write a line, and I'd say, "This, God, this is going to be a humongous laugh." I'm talking aloud as I'm writing because I want to hear what it sounds like in the mouths of the actors. You can hear it.

You do that with all the plays?
Yeah. I don't realize it, I try to keep it low, but my family can hear me mumbling away. But it didn't happen when I was writing this book, because I wasn't reading it aloud to somebody.

Do you visualize a play in performance, too?
Oh, yeah. And that's why it's easier for me to write for the theater, which it isn't for most people. Most writers I know would rather write for the screen. But what I picture is the audience. I don't care what seat you're sitting in, way over to the side, this side, upstairs, there's still that proscenium, so that's the view you're going to get. Whereas the film, they come and they shoot from this side, from above, underneath, not even that character, they're on this character, and in the editing process, they break up the music. I always hear a certain kind of music, not literal music, but the music of the words; there's a certain flow to them. I've had actors like Jack Lemmon say it doesn't happen hardly with any writer he works with. "If you leave out an *and*, an *if*, or a *but*," he says, "it doesn't make much difference to the speech, but when you hear it, something is missing."

Lemmon is quite a cerebral actor, isn't he? He can really articulate the craft.
Oh, yeah, he can. He's wonderful. Mercedes Ruehl, when we were doing *Lost in Yonkers*, came to me when we were in previews— we had done the play for eight weeks on the road already, at the University of North Carolina and then in Washington—and she said, "I beg of you, Neil, if you would just take this one line out of the speech. I think it hurts what she's trying to say." She gave me five different reasons. I said, "Mercedes, try it tonight, and you know, if you're more comfortable with it, then fine, leave it out." So she did

the speech that night, and she didn't take the line out. And I came to her and said, "Why didn't you take it out." She said, "I missed it. I felt the music was wrong without it."

That must make you feel—
Well, you feel wonderful about that.

You say in the book that you've only written two plays for a specific actor in mind.
No, I wrote two films with actors in mind that I knew I would get, because when you're doing a film, you're only doing it for these two actors. But when you're writing a play, you're hoping fifty years from now that there will be all kinds of people doing this play. I tend to think much more of the character as a real character when I'm doing it as a play than I do when I'm writing a film, which sometimes can hurt it, because I'm thinking of a personality, because I know, especially in this day and age, that if I go to a studio with a film that I'm writing, they're going to say, "Well, we'll limit it to the kind of actors we can get for this part. We can't get a box-office actor for this." So they're not as interested in that film, which might change your mind about the kind of movie you want to do. That was not the case twenty-five years ago when a movie cost about $2 million or $3 million to do.

You can't even get a supporting actor today for that money.
That's right.

When you're writing a play, do you have a sense of what the character looks like? Is there a generic character in mind?
Yes, there is. There is, and when they come for auditions, you say, "That's it!" When you see them coming in to read, you say, "Oh God, please let this person read well, because that's exactly what I'm looking for in the type," and it's about fifty-fifty when it works out. It doesn't even work out that often. The performance takes over what they do.

There are some wonderful moments in this book. That story you tell of Dustin Hoffman, when he learns he has the *Graduate* role, and his wife takes the phone—

He told me that story. I would never tell it if I had heard it from someone else.

But he knew it immediately—she knew it immediately—I guess.

It's like what I wrote later on in the book. The opening night of my first play, *Come Blow Your Horn*, Joan, who was the most supporting person you could imagine, had a fight with me that night. I realized she felt that something was going to change us because the play might be successful. And the fact that it was, it was wonderful. And then there was the other side of the coin, how she protected me later on when I did *The Gingerbread Lady*, and the man from *Life* magazine came to the phone and wanted to listen to the reviews coming in. She shoved him across the room, and she was small. I mean, I just cheered for her. It was great.

And buying the place in Pound Ridge?

I was lucky that I could afford it. I felt absolutely helpless in being able to do nothing for Joan when she was dying from cancer. And also, because I was just trying to keep things from her. In buying that house, I knew she would love to be there, because she thought she would be all right.

But the doctor who did the operation, the biopsy on the leg, he said, "No, no way." I don't even think they had chemotherapy then. I don't even know if they would have given it to her then. I don't know.

Do you have favorites among your works?

Well, I never understood what favorite means. Do I like a play better, and for what reason do I like that play better? So, it always has to do with did I have a good time doing that play? Was the writing experience good? Were the actors that I worked with fun?

I've done plays where I've hated every minute of being there, I had trouble with the director, and then the play came out all right. But I think *Lost in Yonkers* is the best play that I've written. They're like your children. You don't pick favorites.

There are some I disfavor. I mean, I don't like them. I think, "God, I did a lousy job with this." Not that I could have done a good job. I think it's written on the wall already about the play. I feel when I sit down to write a play, I usually say this to myself: "If you write this to the best of your ability, how good could it be?" And sometimes the answer is, "It could be pretty good," and sometimes, "It could be incredible." And so you have to resist the temptation to write the one that's going to be just pretty good, because it's going to be an easier play to write. I wrote a couple where I knew they weren't going to be hits at all, but I felt the need to write them, which I think I talk about in the book. One was *God's Favorite*, because it was something that would be cathartic for me, to get out my anger towards why Joan died, and the other was *The Good Doctor*, because I wrote that while Joan was sick, and I had to keep myself busy that summer.

To do that and to be funny at the same time, I don't know how you do it.

Well, there's something that happens, and I've never been able to figure it out, either. Joan was in the bedroom, and I was in this room here, and the minute I go into that world, I'm in there, and it has to be broken by something. I just don't think about what's waiting on the other side. I knew that if I didn't just keep writing every day, she was going to suspect something: "What's the matter? Why aren't you working?" And she was making somewhat of a recovery then. The radiation reduced the tumor. So I felt, well, maybe she'll be all right, and I kept writing.

Do you enter a kind of zone when you're writing?

You mean the figurative?

Yeah.

Yeah. I've written in the dentist's office, waiting to go in. If I'm driving, going to the dentist's office, my mind is working on what I've been writing that morning. God, I want to hold on to those couple of lines, so I've brought the pad with me. Sometimes I'll just write it on a magazine and take it with me. But I am in a zone. I've heard for so long how lonely it is for writers. I've never felt that. I've never felt, my God, I'm alone in this room, I wish there were somebody here with me, I wish there was someone who was going to call me. It's just a place I like to be.

Do you see your plays as a corpus? I mean, if we really want to know about your life fifty years from now, one hundred years from now, do you think that anybody who reads your plays will get a sense of who you are?

Some. Paddy Chayefsky said to me that *Prisoner of Second Avenue* will give a very clear picture of what New York City and maybe America was like at that particular time, because it's right at the period when drugs started to proliferate and crime started to hit the big cities, and that's what that play was about. The characters were robbed right in their house, everything about it was grim, and yet somehow I managed to find some humor in it. *The Odd Couple*, too, I guess, but *The Odd Couple* is very universal. That will go on for years and years because it's such a universal subject.

The title, actually, like *Catch-22* and *The Right Stuff*, has an idiomatic quality to it.

Oh, it has, but it was in our language first. I just used it, and it's sort of taken on a new meaning. I purposely do that sometimes. I take things from the language that sometimes sound like something we heard, like *Last of the Red Hot Lovers*. That was a play on what Sophie Tucker used to call the last of the red hot mommas, since this man was anything but last of the red hot lovers, he was not a lover at all, it seemed like such an ironic title. *Prisoner of Second Avenue* was a good title because it gave a perfect image of what this man was going through, because he lost his job at the age of forty-eight, and his wife went out and went back to the job that she used to have that she quit to raise her daughters. He knew how many steps around the corners of the rooms there were. The title is very important. Sometimes, when I don't get a good title, it means I don't know what the play is really about. I had this title way before I ever wrote the book, because I feel my life is about rewrites, not only in terms of the rewrites I actually do, but the way I've had to rewrite my life based on the circumstances that have happened.

That's a wonderful quote. This could almost be a primer for prospective playwrights.

Well, that's what Jonathan Yardley said—this should be required reading for prospective playwrights.

Did he say that?

Yeah. I do give the sequence of things from the beginning to the end, as I was learning it. I didn't want to keep it strictly that. I didn't want it to be a primer.

You're not dropping names.

They were all part of my learning process.

I love that Jerry Lewis story.

I'll never forget that. He said, "You're the first writer I've ever met who didn't mind cutting something." I said, "Well, why would I want to leave it in when we both know it's not working? I'm glad to get it out." Finding which eight minutes to cut from the TV show was easy for me because I had heard it in the rehearsal and said, "This doesn't work, and this doesn't work." So, as I said at the end of that chapter, I was sure learning how to rewrite, even though I didn't know how to write yet.

What's funny for me about Jerry Lewis is that you laugh at him in spite of yourself?

Right, because I knew it was the lowest common denominator of humor, but it also appealed to that part of me which likes it. Listen, the whole country was Jerry Lewis fans at that time.

All these different plays you've been talking about, there is a poignancy about them, and we're talking about levels of humor. Do you have a philosophy on humor? Is it possible for you to go out and write a very serious drama without any laughs?

I doubt it. I've thought about that, and people have asked me about that. And I say somehow the humor would come in because I see humor in certain kinds of situations. Sometimes I'm not always aware where the humor is. In other words, I'm not always writing jokes, because if you take them out of context, they're not very funny.

When Mike Nichols and I were doing *Plaza Suite*, we were in Boston trying it out at the Colonial. We felt that the first piece had some humor in it, and it turns dark when the wife finds out that the husband is probably having an affair with the secretary and, in fact, he is. But the things that she said back to him had humor to them, but they weren't jokes. But we didn't want the audience to laugh, and they kept laughing. Mike and I went in and we started taking out every laugh, and they found other places to laugh, because I think it made them feel very uncomfortable.

Do people ask you about writing serious plays?

Lost in Yonkers is a serious play. There's humor in it, that's the strangest kind of humor, and I thought it was the best character writing I had done. It was the character of Bella, who was emotionally retarded by the way her mother had stilted her growth. She wants to tell the family that she has met somebody who she wants to marry and open a restaurant with. And he—this man—has more of a physical problem, I would say, in terms of his retardation.

It's so difficult for her to tell them that she's planned it all out. When someone sits down, she says, "No, no, no. You don't sit there, you sit over here," and Jack says, "You have to sit over here," and the audience laughs their way through it. It was funny. I knew it was funny. All four children are dysfunctional, one way or the other. One of them had a voice problem, she couldn't breathe properly because she was nervous about her mother all the time. She had to say the words either on the intake or the out-take, or out-breath. Audiences would laugh, and I knew they would laugh, and I knew that it was disrespectful to laugh, and I think they felt guilty about it. I think that sometimes it's the duty of a playwright to make the audience uncomfortable about something. But that's not something that necessarily makes a hit, because they don't want to feel uncomfortable. They don't want you to do that in a play, and yet, that became the most successful play for me, in terms of praise, for want of a better word.

What advice would you give to young playwrights?

If they're really serious about writing plays, and knowing that they're not going to make much money out of it unless they become successful, then the only advice is that you just have to do it out of your own passion and need to do it. There's no general advice you give in terms of the writing itself. You have to go your own way. I broke a lot of rules and laws when I first started doing it. I try to sometimes discourage someone. I say, "If I can discourage you, and you quit, then you aren't meant to be a playwright." I know what the odds are. The theater is not the primary source of entertainment anymore. You have to realize it's all about movies and television, and if you still want to do it, you must do it.

Do you think of people reading what you write, when you write plays?

They probably read them now more than see them, because it's easier for them to get it. They can get the Samuel French editions.

So they do read them. They have readings of them. People sit around the living room and read them; they each take a part.

It never seemed that you were motivated to be a writer of hardcover books.

No. I spent my youth reading books. I read tons of books. But I was always taken by the theater. The theater was so glamorous then, back in the Fifties when I was going. Even in the Forties, there'd be thirty plays on Broadway, and every year there would be all new plays. You went to see the good ones and the bad ones, and I was slowly learning about it, even though I didn't know that was what I was doing. I was just blown away the first time I saw *A Streetcar Named Desire* with Brando. I said, "Wow, they're breaking all the rules. Here's a guy who's mumbling up on the stage."

Calvin Trillin

Interviewed in Boston on May 23, 1996, for Messages From My Father.

If pressed to offer one word that best describes his late father's personality, the noted *New Yorker* writer Calvin Trillin probably would choose "normal," although "ordinary" and "decent" would apply just as nicely.

Indeed, if any single quality shines through every paragraph of *Messages from My Father*, it is the unfailing propriety with which Abe Trillin comported himself through the sixty years of his life, spent mostly as a grocer, restaurateur, and keeper of a small residential hotel in Kansas City, Missouri.

"I suppose it is somewhat embarrassing to write about your family when it wasn't really dysfunctional," Trillin said jokingly during a recent interview. "But I guess that raises a valid question, doesn't it? Why would anyone want to read about something as mundane as a person who was nothing more than what he was?"

The answer should become clear to anyone who picks up Trillin's tautly crafted memoir and reads it through to the end. "This book is not just about a simple man who got up and went to work every morning, and it's not just about a man who had no pretensions about himself," Trillin emphasized. "It's actually about being a parent and about transmitting values to your children."

Not surprisingly, *Messages from My Father* is dedicated to Abigail Trillin and Sarah Stewart Trillin, neither of whom were alive when their grandfather died twenty-nine years ago, but who are "precisely the granddaughters Abe Trillin would have wanted," their father writes.

A skilled journalist who has written hundreds of literary profiles, essays, columns, and humor pieces over the years for the *New Yorker*, the *Nation*, and *Time*, and published nineteen books as well, Trillin decided for this project to rely mostly on memory, not his reporting skills. A shorter version of *Messages from My Father* was first published in the *New Yorker* two years ago.

"At the time of the *New Yorker* piece, I honestly didn't think I knew enough to write a book about my father, but as it turned out, I was able to add about 40 percent. I think I probably had a lot of information and memories and thoughts about this in the crevices of my mind that I didn't realize I had, and actually, every time I got it back from my editor, I kept adding more and more."

Born near Kiev, in Ukraine, young Abe Trilinsky sailed to America with his family when he was two, and entered the United States in 1907 at Galveston, Texas, not New York, where the vast majority of European immigrants had their first sightings of the New World.

"How did this family—a family indistinguishable from thousands of other poor Eastern European Jewish families saying their farewells to the czar, a family that could have been expected to fetch up on, say, Delancey Street—land in Galveston?" Trillin wonders. "Could it have been stubbornness?"

One of Abe Trillin's more endearing family traits, it turns out, was his stubbornness. He also was modest, neat, scrupulously honest, funny in a wry, self-effacing way, and firmly resolved that his son work hard, go to Yale—indeed, it had to be Yale—and find success and satisfaction as a fully assimilated American with a solid code of Midwestern ethics.

Skilled at gin rummy, pinochle, and poker, Abe Trillin's other hobbies included collecting Yiddish curses and composing the kind of silly rhyming couplets his son would write years later for the

Nation and gather in a 1994 book titled *Deadline Poet*. The elder Trillin's keenest aspiration was to settle in California and open up the kind of no-frills restaurant he ran for a few years in Kansas City. Lingering heart disease kept him close to Kansas City, however, and his death, in 1967, did not come unexpectedly. His son Calvin was thirty-one at the time, married, living in New York, and already embarked on what would become a distinguished writing career.

"So many people of my father's generation are unappreciated in so many ways," Trillin said. "My father worked for years in the grocery business, which he hated from the beginning, so I wouldn't have to be a grocer. It was very clear that my father sort of planned me, and it seems good that my girls know that who they are didn't just happen either, that somebody actually planned for me to be there for them."

Trillin was raised to believe that there was "no restriction on what I could do," and he described the "messages" he received from his father as principles passed on subtly, often in a kind of code which he has tried to convey in similar fashion to his daughters.

"When my daughters were growing up, I had the luxury of spending a lot more time with them than my father had been able to spend with me," he writes. "If I take a long car ride with one of them, there is a lot of talk, but not much of it is terribly personal."

Like their father before them, Abigail and Sarah Stewart Trillin attended Yale and earned degrees. While unable to "isolate the theme" of how he and his wife, Alice, went about raising their daughters in a Greenwich Village brownstone, Trillin does allow that he did not want their formative years "to be as different from my upbringing as it seemed to be," and that if there is, in fact, a theme to be discerned, it is this: "Despite all evidence to the contrary, you are being raised in Kansas City."

John Updike

Interviewed in Boston on October 28, 1996, for Golf Dreams.

When the writer John Updike is driving little white balls off a golf tee, the furthest thing from his mind is whether or not this obsessive exercise has anything to do with creating meaningful literature.

"One of the reasons I play golf is that it gets me away from writing and literary politics, and the rather claustrophobic world of the printed page," the prolific author of forty-six books, seventeen of them elegantly crafted novels, said during a recent interview in Boston.

Yet our talk, aptly enough, was occasioned by the release of *Golf Dreams*, a new collection of thirty "scattered" pieces Updike has written over the years about the diversion he sometimes feels has "stolen my life away." A native of Shillington, Pennsylvania, the sixty-four-year-old man of letters has lived for the past four decades in Beverly Farms, Massachusetts, a coastal community just north of Boston. He is best known by thousands of readers as creator of the four Harry "Rabbit" Angstrom novels (*Rabbit, Run*; *Rabbit Redux*; *Rabbit Is Rich*; and *Rabbit at Rest*), and other contemporary classics such as *The Poorhouse Fair*, *The Centaur*, *Couples*, and *The Witches of Eastwick*.

Updike's honors include two Pulitzer Prizes, two National Book Critics Circle Awards, the National Book Award, the American

Book Award, and the Howells Medal, and he is equally adept at writing short stories, essays, criticism, and poetry as he is at shaping sophisticated novels; his oeuvre also includes *Self-Consciousness*, a memoir, *Buchanan Dying*, a play, and five children's books.

Golf Dreams developed more or less by happenstance, Updike acknowledged. "The book wouldn't exist if *Golf Digest* hadn't invited me to write an annual essay on golf some years ago," although he has done a few fictional treatments of the game as part of larger works. In addition to the *Golf Digest* magazine articles, the collection includes excerpts from the novels *Rabbit, Run*; *Rabbit at Rest*; and *A Month of Sundays*, a short story written in the 1950s, as well as pieces that first appeared in the *New Yorker* and other publications.

Updike's romance with the sport began in 1954, not long after he graduated summa cum laude from Harvard College and returned home from a year of study at Oxford University. "When you're a kid, you have wimps who don't do sports at all, or you have jocks who can do them all very nicely, and I was really somewhere in between," he recalled. "I wasn't very good at sports, but I did like athletic endeavors, and I played a lot of alley basketball, a lot of touch football, a lot of vacant-lot baseball, so the sensations of all these sports were real to me, even though I never ascended the heights. I wasn't what my father used to call a 'natural.' He was a public-school teacher and kind of a fatalist about performance—academics as well as sports. In his view, you either had it or you didn't."

Nevertheless, as he got older, Updike found golf particularly seductive. "For me to have some sport I could do as an adult, not lose all the time, win some of the time, and be better than some people, if worse than others—all that is kind of meaningful to me," he said.

"In a way, it has kind of kept me in touch with my physical self. The simplicity and difficulty of the swing, all that loomed to me as exciting, mystical even. So it became something that interested me, and it turned out that I wanted to write about it after all."

With a subtle blend of dry wit and graceful language, Updike has loosely structured *Golf Dreams* around "learning," "playing," and "loving" the game. The title piece has pride of place in the collection, and alternates between moods of fantasy and nightmare on the fairways. "In the winter, you get this golf hunger, and it begins to enter your dreams," Updike explained. "You always accept the course in a golf dream. However outrageously difficult it is, whether you're hitting off a table or trying to get the ball into a thimble, you always doggedly accept it as the way you do on a real golf course."

He paused momentarily before putting the matter into further context. "It is true, that like sex, if you go without golf for a while, you begin to dream about it, and that has been the case with me."

As one of the truly great fiction writers of his generation, Updike has no trouble describing golf in metaphoric terms. "It teaches you about life, it teaches you about yourself," he said. "Golf doesn't let you kid yourself. In a way, it's a lot of what life is not like now, in a crowded world. It offers you space, it allows kind of a return to the hunter self. Golf courses and cemeteries are among the last places that continue to hold open land for us, at least here in the Northeast."

Away from the golf course, Updike is a tireless worker, and rarely a year goes by without one book or other issuing forth from his imagination. Each of his four Rabbit books appeared at the start of a new decade, but with the death of Harry Angstrom in *Rabbit at Rest* six years ago, he has been forced to modify his routine.

"It's sort of scary now, as I approach the time when I would be beginning yet another Rabbit novel, to realize that I've pretty well precluded the possibility of any sequel," he said, although he holds out the prospect of bringing back Henry Bech, a writer not a lot unlike himself who appeared in two collections of stories, *Bech: A Book* and *Bech Is Back*.

"I love those Bech stories, I think they were among my crispest," he said. "Unlike Rabbit, Henry Bech was a character who was articulate, and there was no thought you could have that you couldn't assign to him. He was a sort of thinking intellectual who offered himself as a receptacle for me."

By "receptacle," of course, Updike means a character he can use as something of an alter ego. "You want somebody who's enough unlike you that it's fun to be imagining yourself in his skin, or her skin, but also somebody to which you can feel simpatico and have some identification with," he concluded. "That's the magic word—identification."

It is that very word, in fact, that will apply to the legions of fairway aficionados who dip into this agreeable book about a shared passion.

Kurt Vonnegut

Interviewed in Boston on September 25, 1997, for Timequake.

Is this really your last book?
Yes, I think so.

Are you tired of writing?
I am completely in print. My publishing history has been most agreeable. I continue to say everything I ever wanted to say. I have been straining all of my life to communicate something, and I think the messages have all got through.

Do you think that this has something to do with the difficulty that you had with this novel?
It took me a while to figure out what it should be, which is the last chapter in one big book rather than a freestanding piece of work. But it also happens that I just didn't like the story. It wasn't my kind of story. I wasn't that interested in it.

Then why didn't you just chuck it?
I did chuck it.

But it took you ten years to come to that conclusion?
That's the way it goes.

Was there some point along the way where you said this just isn't working?

Of course that happened. The book was accepted. It was finished. And it was in the Putnam catalogue, and I said I don't like it. So I started all over again. So what we have here is a nice coda, and what the hell. How many authors live to be seventy-five and get to look back at everything they did?

Looking back at it now, it is a complete body of work that now has boundaries. Do you see it as a corpus?

Yes, I do. I see it as organic with my life. It could have been quite separate, you know. I could have written a bunch of detective stories or whatever, which would have been little gems. It turns out retrospectively to be quite personal.

Do you think it is necessary, then—to truly understand you—that we must read the body of work?

This book will make no sense to anyone who hasn't read at least one other book of mine. The mail I get often is, "I have read everything you have ever written." That is very nice to hear. But it is an accident. You can't create that. You can't just make it happen. One time I was down in the Virgin Islands and papers were blowing by, pages out of a book, and I started chasing it. I got it all piled up against a shrub and it was a memoir by André Gide, who I had never read before, and Christ, I was able to gather up this book and read it on the beach. I had to read it at that point and find out what it was. The whole thing wasn't there, but what I did read was quite interesting. And it was fun chasing the pages.

Styron has been quite eloquent on the subject. He said the great Russian novels were written for a very small audience because it was not a literate nation at that time, but it was enough. We are all money crazy and fame crazy now, but maybe there is just going to be a small audience. But it still is an audience. And it ought to be respected as such and enjoyed as such. What I have said is that the Jeffersonian dream of a literate electorate is crazy. It is like expecting everyone to play the French horn, because it is hard to read. *Slaughterhouse Five* is taught in high school, and you know these kids are having trouble. I mean the story isn't sequential; all of a sudden we are twenty years ago, and they say "Hey, come on. Give me a break. You know I am paying attention, and you are saying something and meaning another? Come on."

You say straight out in this book that Kilgore Trout is your alter ego. Explain to me what an alter ego is to you.
    Well, in this case, he is the science fiction writer I might have been because some people get hooked on that and are really pretty good writers from time to time. I taught at the Iowa Writers Workshop for two years, 1965 and 1966, and among my students were John Irving, who has done reasonably well since then, and Gail Godwin and John Casey, who won a National Book Award, and a local boy, Andre Dubus. These people were all mature, incidentally, they had already had love affairs and had their hearts broken and had kids, so they really had a lot to write about. They were really an interesting bunch. At one point, I told them to go to the Iowa City Public Library and find novels that hadn't been taken out for years and see whether they were any good or not—unknown names, not Sinclair Lewis or anything like that. They found some swell books. I have always been dependent on my liberal arts friends to find out what to read. And here I am, I will soon be seventy-five, and I have my block knocked off by a book I had heard about just a month ago. A friend said, "You know, I just read your book, and you are a clone of Erasmus of Rotterdam." And so he loaned me his copy of *In Praise of Folly*. Jesus Christ, he was right.
    He's very interesting because he was a translator of different works, the Bible and all that, a great biblical scholar. You can't detect that he's a skeptic about Christianity and about the Holy Scriptures, but one thing he does do, as a scholar, is say that the Trinity is a fraud. There's no justification whatsoever for it in scriptures. It was interpolated many years later. That took balls. I'm a skeptic, of course.

I was raised as an atheist by good people who were atheists. I read in Will and Ariel Durant's book on the Middle Ages that there were outspoken skeptics, but they were upper class. They were protected while other people were getting burned at the stake. You show me the torture instruments, and I'll apologize for anything you ask!

Is there anything with your work that you would go back and tinker with if you had the chance?

There are mistakes, tactical mistakes. I have said to students that whatever you write—a short story or a novel, I don't care what it is—it has to be like an egg. Everything that is necessary for life is inside that shell. With this last book, I realized that the shell that had enclosed the whole thing of my work was cracked.

One of your reviewers has said that *Timequake* is a clever way to do a memoir as novel and novel as memoir. How do you see it?

That is not my problem. It is not even your problem. I spoke at Ohio Wesleyan three nights ago, and one person said, "Several people have called you a post-modernist. Do you accept this?" And I didn't have a clue. I said it is like a character in Molière who is delighted to find out he is writing prose. He hadn't realized it before.

I was born in 1922, and I was fortunate to have writers ahead of me who were breaking all sorts of ground: Dos Passos and Steinbeck and Erskine Caldwell, and so forth.

It is interesting that you are naming all American writers here?

You people in New York and Boston face Europe. My center of gravity is Chicago. We don't look across the Atlantic. I will tell you a book that really knocked my block off was the *Spoon River Anthology*.

Is *Slaughterhouse-Five* the defining work for you?

It was reviewed on the front page of the *New York Times*, and I had been ignored up to then. *Cat's Cradle* was never reviewed. *Mother Night* was never reviewed. *Sirens of Titan* was never reviewed.

As far as the *Times* was concerned, you were an unknown writer up to the arrival of that book.

I was operating in a negligible genre supposedly: science fiction for seventeen-year-olds. They weren't reading me, the critics at the *Times* or *Newsweek* or *Time* magazine or the *New York Review of Books*. They had enough to read already.

I do love the epigraph to *Timequake*: "All persons living and dead are purely coincidental." And also you dedicate the book to your publisher, Seymour Lawrence.

He was at the *Atlantic Monthly Press* for a long time, but he had his office there on the edge of the Boston Public Garden. I used to visit him there. He picked up a group of us who, I guess, were defined by our audience. Me and Richard Brautigan and a whole bunch of us. Yeah, I miss Sam. Jesus, he saved my life. I've said I was very lucky, taking advertising jobs and PR jobs. I never represented a product that was lousy or a contemptible dictator. And then I was desperately trying to sell Saabs, and I was an awful car dealer.

Kilgore is safely retired now?

They're all retired now.

So what are you going to do now?

Well, I write a lot of letters, and I keep busy farting around. Some people have no gift for farting around. I do. I can make a day disappear.

What was there about *Slaughterhouse-Five* that finally persuaded the critics that you should be noticed? That you demanded attention?

Sam Lawrence wanted it to happen. He was all excited about it. And people who read it were talking about it. It got a shitty review in *Newsweek*. Some people think if you make jokes, you are not a serious writer. But I can't help it. It's a nice skill to have, to be funny.

Is it hard to be funny?

Not for me. It is nice how much nonsense makes life bearable for us. Please don't be so serious. Paul Engle, who founded the Writers Workshop out in Iowa, said that if we ever got a building, he would put over the doorway, "Don't Take Yourself So Seriously."

Alice Walker

*Interviewed in Boston on October 16, 1998,
for* By the Light of My Father's Smile.

Given the fact that most of Alice Walker's readers are women and acknowledging, also, that she has a reputation in some quarters for being a male-basher in her fiction, the well-known author of *The Color Purple* has one suggestion for people coming to her work for the first time.

"Open-mindedness," the fifty-four-year-old author said unhesitatingly during an interview in Boston that was occasioned by the recent release of her first novel to appear in six years, *By the Light of My Father's Smile*.

"All I ever ask from a reader is to accept that I am entitled to have a different world view, and that you approach me on the basis of, you know, 'Maybe this is just someone who doesn't see things the way I do,'" she explained. "You have to approach writers like me the way you would approach another culture, because I do come from another culture, even though I am in this one. That's what I mean when I say you need open-mindedness."

Not surprisingly, Walker's new book has drawn a striking variety of critical response from reviewers around the country. Some of the opinions are so diverse that a person unfamiliar with her work might swear that different books are being discussed by the reviewers. Consider the following examples:

Anna Mundow in the *New York Daily News* writes that admirers of Walker's books "will be enthralled" with *By the Light of My Father's Smile* and declares it to be the "most distilled expression" of her thinking to date, "as much an incantation as it is a story."

Writing in the *Houston Chronicle*, Joy R. Sewing saw the novel as an ill-conceived "celebration of eros" that is "muddied up with an odd assortment of underdeveloped characters, disjointed metaphors, dizzying jaunts back and forth through time, and spiritual mumbo jumbo."

At the *Boston Globe*, Ellen Clegg describes this novel of an African-American family's awakening experiences while living among a primitive tribe in Mexico as "pared down and powerful, bristling with primary colors and scents," all the while giving "few hints of the agenda-driven didacticism that can occasionally creep into" Walker's writing.

Debra Dickerson in *The Washington Post*: "The problem here is that there are no people, only political vehicles sprinkled with magic and dead men walking."

And Richard Bernstein in the *New York Times*: "Ms. Walker's new novel recounts the interwoven experiences of several women, though the underlying message of the book, hammered home in frequent passages of sophomoric didacticism, is that most men are not very admirable, that sex is spiritual, and that primitive civilizations are morally and sensually superior to technologically advanced ones."

When asked to explain how one writer can manage to elicit so many different reactions with one novel, Walker smiled softly. "You know what? I don't read reviews until at least three months after my books are published, if at all."

Walker said, furthermore, that she always expects "strong reactions on both sides" for her books, "because everything I have written has been very much from my own point of view, and very uncompromising, and so I feel that, lucky for me, I have a very large readership that is very devoted and is willing to try and see what I'm talking about."

Possessing the Secret of Joy, Walker's last novel prior to *By the Light of My Father's Smile*, appeared in 1992, and dealt with what most readers agreed was a radical subject, the brutality of female circumcision as it has been practiced for centuries in areas of Africa and the Middle East.

By far the best known of her eleven books is *The Color Purple*, a landmark in the literature of female oppression and the struggle of black women against racism and violence and the winner of the Pulitzer Prize and National Book Award for 1983. Required reading in many schools, it was the basis of a hugely successful motion picture directed by Steven Spielberg, which also launched the acting careers of Oprah Winfrey and Whoopi Goldberg.

Walker grew up in rural Georgia, the youngest of eight children, and studied literature at Spelman College in Atlanta and Sarah Lawrence College in New York. Now living in northern California, Walker has continued to write and speak out on the issues that have occupied her attention for the past thirty years.

Her work has taken an explicitly New Age turn, a development she makes clear in the acknowledgments she appends to *By the Light of My Father's Smile*. There, she thanks "the Great Spirit of the Universe for regularly carrying me to the edge, permitting me to contemplate the drop, and for holding me well."

The primary intention of the new novel is to pointedly express Walker's world view, and to offer forth what she calls "a celebration" of sexuality. "To deny people the full expression of their sexuality is to deny them a major opportunity for self knowledge and enlightenment, which is the light of knowing who you are," she said.

Given the moralistic and pedantic nature of the book, the question arises as to why she decided to write it as a novel, and not nonfiction. "Fiction is absolutely so wonderful because it permits you to create an object, the novel, in a story, and this object can exist in a way that is distant from the reader," she said.

"Essentially, what you are saying is that this is a work of art, and you study it and feel it at your leisure. And if you have a response, great, and if you don't, fine. You know? Fiction is like that. It really frees you. And it also is the kind of thing that waits for you. If you're not ready for a particular work of fiction at sixteen, or thirty-two, or fifty-seven, wait a few years, and it will be there."

Dorothy West

*Interviewed in Oak Bluffs, Massachusetts,
on February 8, 1995, for The Wedding.*

At eighty-seven, Dorothy West is enjoying all the attention she has been getting lately, not only because she has published her first novel in forty-seven years, but also for being honored as the lone survivor of the Harlem Renaissance, an artistic phenomenon that flourished in the 1920s and '30s with the emergence of black writers and artists celebrating their own culture.

West is the daughter of a former slave. She went to New York City at age eighteen to accept a literary prize she shared with Zora Neale Hurston, the noted folklorist, novelist, memoirist, and anthropologist. West's entry in the 1926 contest, conducted by the Urban League's *Opportunity* magazine, was a short story called "The Typewriter." The following year, she landed a bit part in the original stage production of *Porgy*, the Pulitzer Prize–winning dramatization of a DuBose Heyward novel and the basis for George Gershwin's great folk opera, *Porgy and Bess.*

Because she came from a family of means, West, in 1934, was able to establish an African American literary magazine known as *Challenge*; three years later, with Richard Wright as co-editor, she founded *New Challenge*, a more politically concerned journal that published the work of many black writers. In addition to Hurston and Heyward, West's friends during that time included such luminaries as Langston Hughes, Paul Robeson, Alain Locke, Wallace Thurman, Gwendolyn Bennett, Claude McKay, and the noted poet Countee Porter Cullen.

For more than fifty years, West has lived on the island of Martha's Vineyard, in the fairy-tale town of Oak Bluffs, a community of charming gingerbread cottages, long known as a retreat for successful African Americans. The petite West is full of energy and good will. Her mind is a whirlwind of memories and impressions, and she is eager to share them all. Laughter comes easily for her, though occasionally there is sadness, even tears.

West is a prolific short-story writer whose work is widely anthologized. Her first novel, *The Living Is Easy*, was published in 1948 and set in Oak Bluffs. Despite her advancing years, the recent release of *The Wedding* makes clear that she remains a vibrant literary voice.

Racial politics are very much a factor in the structure of the new novel, but in unexpected and often surprising ways. At the center of the story, which also has an Oak Bluffs setting, is the forthcoming marriage of Shelby Coles, the blue-eyed, fair-skinned daughter of Dr. and Mrs. Clark Coles, a prominent "colored" couple, to a "nameless, faceless" white jazz musician.

The central conflict is caused by the arrival on the island of Lute McNeil, a successful Boston furniture maker of "nut-brown" complexion. He sees winning Shelby, and being accepted by her family, as the crowning accomplishment of his life—a validation of his success—and he is determined to thwart the wedding plans.

Gradations of skin color and perceptions of appearance and reality are themes that are handled with a gentle, deft hand, yet with remarkable economy. West's lucid examination of five generations of cultural heritage, recalled through the recollections of various family members, makes the book a legitimate work of social history.

She was interviewed in a small, shingled house in the Highlands section of town, once her family's summer residence, where she has lived since 1943.

You have been described as the last surviving member of the Harlem Renaissance. How does that make you feel—that you represent the last of an important cultural movement?

The first time I realized that I was the last one from that group still alive was at a dinner they gave for me a while back at Radcliffe College. The woman who introduced me said that Dorothy West is the last person from the Harlem Renaissance still with us and that all the others are gone. Right there, I understood what all the fuss was about, and why these people had come to see me. Everyone else is gone.

Did you have a sense back in the 1920s and '30s that you were taking part in a great cultural and artistic explosion?

We never called what we were doing the Harlem Renaissance; that all came later. What we did know was that something very exciting was going on. People were doing creative things, and it was special because that kind of experience only happens once in history. When I first got to the "Magic City," which is what we called New York back then, I was eighteen, and I never opened my mouth for the longest time. I kept quiet and paid attention. I was just a child, but they were very protective of me.

Your father was a former slave who became tremendously successful as a produce merchant after the Civil War. What kinds of things did he tell you about his childhood?

My father was born into slavery in Virginia, and when freedom came, he was seven years old. He moved north and became known as the "Black Banana King of Boston." My mother was much younger than my father. She was born in North Carolina and came north when she was fourteen. She was one of nineteen children and was known as one of the "Twelve Beauties of Boston." After both my mother and my father were dead, I wondered why I had never asked them certain questions. The truth is that they probably didn't want to talk about it. I cannot tell you how many times I've said, "My God, I never asked my father what it was like to be a slave." That's one of the reasons why I wanted to write this book. My father was born a slave, but he also happened to have blue eyes; therefore, he had to have a little white ancestry. As you know, the book gets into these matters.

Have you ever wondered why your parents allowed their only child to go off alone to New York City?

I have thought about that many times as well. It was my mother who let me go, and I believe I know why. When she was fourteen, her mother let her go north, knowing she might never see her child again, but she let her go because she knew it was for the best. Her mother let her go, and that is why she let me go. I am certain that this is the reason.

I am told you once turned down a proposal of marriage from Countee Cullen, one of your colleagues during the Harlem Renaissance, a gifted poet. Is that true?

Yes, it is. I was afraid to get married. I always wanted to be a writer, you see, from the time I was a little girl. And if I had married him, that dream probably would have ended.

Can you tell us a little bit about how this all started? What forces drove you as a child to become a writer?

I was seven years old when I said to my mother, "May I close the door to my room?" She said I could do that, but she wanted to know why. Children were polite in those days, and we asked permission to do things. Well, I told her I wanted to be alone to think. When I was eleven, I asked her if I could lock the door, and she asked why. I said, "Because now I want to write."

So much of *The Wedding* takes place right here in the town of Oak Bluffs, on Martha's Vineyard, where you have lived since 1943. Can we assume you have drawn on your own life and experiences for the novel?

Yes and no. I was inspired by a lot of things that have happened around me. I can tell you that the book would never have been what it is if there had not been a situation some years ago where a woman and her child were trying to get off the island one Sunday, and the little girl wandered off and got lost. It caused quite a stir. We finally found her, but that came back to me when I was writing the novel, and I used it for a pretty important scene. I always say if there weren't any real people, I don't know how I'd write, because I am a writer, and I have a writer's memory. But once my imagination takes over, it goes off on its own.

I don't want to give away too much of the novel, but you're talking about a very powerful scene at the end of the book where the character Lute is driving around and looking for his lost daughter, and there's a terrible accident that has tragic consequences.

You're right. You know, something happened to me while I was working on that particular chapter; it was the strangest feeling I have ever had. I never will forget it, because this never happened to me before, and it will never happen again. All of a sudden, you see, I was in the book—and I've never been so scared in my life. I remember saying to myself, "Be calm, be calm, be calm," and I remember putting on my coat and hat, and I went out to walk. I was afraid somebody would say something to me, because I was in that world—another world—and then just as quickly I snapped out of it.

You dedicate *The Wedding* to your editor at Doubleday, Jacqueline Kennedy Onassis, who died last year. She had a summer house on the island, about fifteen miles away in Chilmark. Did the two of you get together, when she was staying here, to work on the book?

I'll tell you a cute story about that. You know that I set the book in a part of Oak Bluffs called the Oval. Well there is no oval in town, but if you look outside at my little street, it looks kind of like a little oval, so it happened that one day while I was working on the book, I went outside and looked around, and I said, "Oh, that's an oval." Well, the first day Mrs. Onassis came to see me, she was asking people all around, "Where's the Oval?" She assumed it was a real place, but nobody could tell her where it was, because nobody knew. So she finally said to someone, "Where does Dorothy West live?" and they told her.

The way we worked together, I would do a chapter, send it to her, then she would come back on the following Monday, and we'd talk about it. She'd sit right where you are sitting now and ask me to tell her everything. I'd tell her something, and she would say, "Oh, Dottie, you have to put that in your book."

You have written one other novel, *The Living Is Easy*, which is also set on Martha's Vineyard. That was published in 1948. Why did you wait so long to write another novel?

I didn't wait this long to write another book. The truth is that I did work on another book, but we went through a time there when books by black authors just weren't selling. In fact, there was a contest some years ago, and I got a $1,000 grant, but the time just wasn't right. I felt that if I brought the book out then, the white reviewers would not understand it; they would just clobber it. So I put the book aside, and then the situation got better, and I started *The Wedding*. But I have written more than a hundred stories over the years, and Doubleday is bringing out a collection of them sometime this summer. I must confess, I love my short stories. You'd be amazed at how many schools read my short stories in their classes.

You have lived a tremendously eventful life. How would you like to be remembered?

First of all, I am a Bostonian, and Bostonians are not much accustomed to saying very much about themselves. But I will say that I have a sense of humor about myself and that I always hung in there. I was so serious as a child. I can still hear my mother saying, "You'd better learn to laugh, little girl, you'd better learn to laugh." Before long, I discovered that I like life. I like life—and I love people.

Acknowledgments

I am grateful to Webb Howell, the publisher of *Fine Books & Collections* magazine, for seeing merit in gathering a selection of these pieces and publishing them in this book, and also for the collection of my essays, *Editions & Impressions*, which he published in such an elegant and professional manner three years ago. From the first day Webb introduced himself to me after a talk I gave at the Folger Shakespeare Library in Washington, D. C., in 2003, and invited me to write for the magazine he was about to launch, his word has been rock solid, and I am pleased to express my appreciation to him on this occasion.

It has also been a singular pleasure for me to work with Scott Brown, the founding editor of *Fine Books & Collections*, and the editor of these two books for Fine Books Press. When Webb greenlighted this collection, I went through every column I had written—score one for having kept thorough files over the years—and came up with two hundred pieces I particularly liked. But it was Scott who proposed the selection presented herewith. "It shows all kinds of writers and their approach to craft," he explained, and I agreed with him in every instance. Scott also gets credit for suggesting that we include the verbatim texts of ten of the interviews I conducted, only one of which—the Dorothy West Q & A—has ever appeared in print before. My thanks go out, too, to the many news and feature editors at the newspapers around the country who published my columns over the years, a number of whom became good friends through our work together. They were all wonderful journalists, and it has pained me deeply to see so many of them let go in these days of declining circulations and for reasons that have nothing at all to do with the work they did so well. You gave me an opportunity when I needed it the most, and I am forever grateful.

Finally, of course, is the dedicatee of this book, my wife, Constance Basbanes, who has, indeed, been along for the whole ride. Her judgment and critical acumen are second to none; her support, encouragement, and common sense are ever the saving grace.

Sources

With the exception of Dorothy West, the interviews in this book are all previously unpublished and were transcribed from audiotapes. The essays appeared in a variety of newspapers and magazines, and many were widely syndicated in publications around the United States. The newspapers frequently edited the stories to fit the available space, so whenever possible this book relies on the original manuscripts. In the following cases, however, the essays were transcribed from the best-available published source.

Ambrose, Stephen. "Stephen Ambrose: Annals of American Leadership" in *Publishers Weekly*, January 22, 1996.

Atwood, Margaret. "Margaret Atwood's Newest Book Is Hard to Categorize" in the *Allentown (Pa.) Morning Call*, February 12, 1995.

Baker, Russell. "Russell Baker: The Thoughtful Man Behind the Humorist" in the *Worcester (Mass.) Sunday Telegram*, November 28, 1982.

Clancy, Tom. "Tom Clancy Gets Visit from CIA" in the *Worcester (Mass.) Evening Gazette*, August 17, 1988.

Fitzgerald, Penelope. "Taking Tea with Toast of Literary World; British Novelist Penelope Fitzgerald Says She Is Floored by U.S. Award" in the *Cleveland Plain Dealer*, April 12, 1998.

Ford, Richard. "Moving Around Affords Richard Ford 'Independence'" in the Allentown (Pa.) Morning Call, July 23, 1995.

Gordimer, Nadine. "S. African Novelist Doesn't Write to Be Political" in the *Allentown (Pa.) Morning Call*, December 25, 1994.

Gordon, Noah. "Noah Gordon: Famous Abroad, On the Rise Here" in *Publishers Weekly*, April 1, 1996.

Heller, Joseph. "'God Knows,'" It's Joseph Heller" in the *Worcester (Mass.) Evening Gazette*, October 3, 1984.

Irving, John. "For John Irving, 'Circus' Is a Novel Kind of Freak Show" in the *Allentown (Pa.) Morning Call*, September 10, 1994.

L'Amour, Louis. "Novelist's Latest Frontier: 25 Million More Readers" in the *Worcester (Mass.) Sunday Telegram*, August 22, 1982.

La Plante, Lynda. "Authenticity a Prerequisite for This Award-winning Author" in the *Worcester (Mass.) Telegram and Gazette*, May 8, 1996.

Lessing, Doris. "Lessing Writing Autobiography to Get Story Right" in the *Wisconsin State Journal* (Madison), December 25, 1994.

Miller, Arthur. "Arthur Miller: From Fitful Start to Modern Literary Giant" in the *Worcester (Mass.) Sunday Telegram*, March 27, 1988.

Oe, Kenzaburo. "During Time Off, Celebrated Writer Hopes to Create New Literary Form" in the *Columbus (Ohio) Dispatch*, August 17, 1995.

Paley, Grace. "'Collected Stories' Reflects Growth of Paley's Career" in the *Worcester (Mass.) Telegram and Gazette*, June 8, 1994.

Trillin, Calvin. "Trillin's Memoir Transmits Values of Beloved Father" in the *Worcester (Mass.) Telegram & Gazette*, June 12, 1996.

West, Dorothy. "Another Renaissance for Dorothy West" in the *Minneapolis Star-Tribune*, April 10, 1995.